Making any necessary changes to your home will literally transform your life, improving it in every possible way.

—Richard Webster

In his book *The Importance of Living,* Lin Yutang (1895–1976) writes that we should arrange our lives to ensure that we find the greatest amount of happiness.

You can find happiness, and make it a natural and lasting part of your life, with the ancient Chinese art of feng shui— *Feng Shui for Success & Happiness* shows you how. The basic ideas are very simple and can easily be put into place in your home. Learn about the principles for successful living: ch'i, the pa-kua, the five elements, the nine sectors, and fortunate and unfortunate directions.

Happiness and good fortune mean different things to different people. By applying proven feng shui techniques in your home, you can improve health, attract or rekindle love, strengthen spirituality, and create prosperity for yourself and your household.

Arrange your life around the principles of feng shui, and whether you live in a small apartment or a grand mansion, you'll find there's room for greater happiness and success!

About the Author

Richard Webster was born in New Zealand in 1946, where he still resides. He travels widely every year, lecturing and conducting workshops on psychic subjects around the world. He has written many books, mainly on psychic subjects, and also writes monthly magazine columns.

Richard is married with three children. His family is very supportive of his occupation, but his oldest son, after watching his father's career, has decided to become an accountant.

To Write to the Author

If you wish to contact the author or would like more information about this book, please write to the author in care of Llewellyn Worldwide, and we will forward your request. Both the author and publisher appreciate hearing from you. Llewellyn Worldwide cannot guarantee that every letter written to the author can be answered, but all will be forwarded. Please write to:

Richard Webster
℅ Llewellyn Worldwide
P.O. Box 64383, Dept. K815-X
St. Paul, MN 55164-0383, U.S.A.

Please enclose a self-addressed, stamped envelope for reply, or $1.00 to cover costs. If outside the U.S.A., enclose international postal reply coupon.

FENG
SHUI
for
Success &
Happiness

RICHARD
WEBSTER

1999
Llewellyn Publications
St. Paul, Minnesota 55164-0383
U.S.A.

FIRST EDITION
Second Printing, 1999

Book design: Amy Rost
Cover design: Tom Grewe
Interior illustrations: Jeannie Ferguson
Typesetting and editing: Michael Maupin

Library of Congress Cataloging-in-Publication Data
Webster, Richard, 1946–
    Feng shui for success & happiness / Richard Webster.
        p.   cm.
    Includes bibliographical references and index
    ISBN 1-56718-815-X
    1. Feng-shui.   I. Title.   II. Title: Feng shui for success and
happiness.
BF1779.F4W438   1999
133.3'337—dc21   99-12895
                                                            CIP

Llewellyn Publications
A Division of Llewellyn Worldwide, Ltd.
P.O. Box 64383, Dept. K815-X
St. Paul, Minnesota 55164-0383

♻ Printed in the United States of America on recycled paper

Other Books by Richard Webster

Dedication

For Tai Lau (1903 – 1998)
The master who refused to call himself a master

Contents

Introduction

One joy scatters a hundred griefs.

—Chinese proverb

Many years ago, a wise man gave me the secret of happiness. It was incredibly simple and at the same time extremely profound. "If you want to be happy," he told me, "Be happy!"

This was excellent advice, and I have tried to follow it ever since. However, it is not always easy to remain happy when your environment works against you. I have friends who lived close to a major airport for three years. Their home was beautiful and perfect for their needs, but the constant noise of planes taking off and landing ultimately forced them to move.

Other people I know live on the bend of a major road. All night long their home is swept by the headlights of cars using the road. They suffered from lack of sleep for months, until they erected a large wall to shield them from the headlight beams. Although they did not know it at the time, they had used a common feng shui remedy to solve their problem.

Our friends resolved their problem by moving to a new house, while the other couple made their problem disappear. However, neither family would ever have been completely happy if they had stayed where they were, and simply tried to be happy.

Fortunately, there is a way to live in harmony with your environment. It is the ancient Chinese art of feng shui, which, when applied, can give you a life of happiness, contentment, and abundance. The term "feng shui" means "wind and water." Five thousand years ago, the Chinese discovered that life was much more pleasant living in a house that faced south, with hills behind it to provide protection from the cold north winds, and with gently flowing water in front. From this beginning, the art and science of feng shui evolved through a process of experimentation, and today it has spread around the world and is more popular than ever before.

The Chinese have always been interested in symbols that represent good fortune. For the Chinese, good fortune is not limited to some chance occurrence of luck, such as winning a lottery. It also includes...

...a long and healthy life
...many male children to carry on the family line
...a good reputation
...material prosperity
...a happy marriage
...good friends
...a successful career
...honor and respect from others

Of course, living in the Western world, you may not want all of these Chinese indicators of good fortune. Naturally, a large number of people choose to live on their own, and many choose not to have children. You can be perfectly happy without a partner or children of either sex. It depends entirely on what you want. Happiness and good fortune mean different things to different people.

In fact, it is virtually impossible to define happiness. Joseph Spence wrote: "The happiness of life is so nice a thing that, like the sensitive plant, it shrinks away, even upon thinking of it."[1] I am supremely happy lying in bed with a good book. My brother-in-law is happiest while doing maintenance work on his home. I do not enjoy painting and household repair work, and I doubt if he would get much pleasure from reading a book in bed. Yet we are both equally as happy when doing something that we enjoy.

In his book *The Importance of Living*, Lin Yutang (1895 –1976), argues that the purpose of life is to enjoy it.[2] Rather than finding a purpose, he says, we should arrange our lives to ensure that we can find the greatest amount of happiness.

Happiness is usually found in the small things. A pleasant view, a lazy morning in bed, a picnic, or a bottle of wine shared with a friend can often bring more happiness than receiving a large pay raise or award. Of course, when we are happy, we never stop to analyze the feeling. We simply *enjoy* it.

Chin Shengt'an, a well-known seventeenth-century Chinese critic, was once trapped by bad weather in a temple for ten days. While there, he made a list of thirty-three happy moments, all of which were minor incidents. They included cutting open a ripe watermelon on a summer's afternoon, opening a window to let a wasp out, and suddenly realizing that a gentle snow is falling.

Shortly before he died, Lord Byron told a friend that he had been happy for only three hours in his whole life.[3] A melancholy disposition may be useful to a poet who can express his or her emotions on paper, but to achieve merely three hours of happiness over a lifetime is tragic.

I would much rather have the outlook of Chin Shengt'an than that of Lord Byron. Certainly, his approach of finding pleasure in small things is an excellent recipe for happiness.

In this book you will learn how to activate different parts of your home, be it a one-room apartment or a large mansion, to improve your environment and to achieve happiness, contentment, and abundance.

1

Feng Shui and Happiness

The sense of existence is the greatest happiness.[1]

—Benjamin Disraeli

Just as in other parts of the world, life in China five thousand years ago was difficult. Most people lived close to rivers and the sea, and lived on a diet of fish and rice. They worked hard, but were for the most part, happy. Confucius (551 B.C.E.–479 B.C.E.), the famous Chinese philosopher, gave profound advice when he said: "With coarse rice to eat, with only water to drink, and my bended arm for a pillow, I am happy."[2] He implies that complete happiness comes from a rich inner life, rather than from material possessions.

Of course, in Confucius' time, the serfs constantly suffered from lack of food, and the Chinese character for happiness (*fu*) is derived from the idea of a satisfied stomach. People who were not hungry were much more likely to be happy than the poorest peasants who were always craving more food.

Hungry or not, the people of this time noticed that different environments had a direct bearing on happiness, contentment, and even luck. Later on, these factors would become known as feng shui, the art of living in harmony with the earth.

No one knows exactly how or when feng shui began. According to legend, it began when a large tortoise crawled out of the Yellow River some five thousand years ago while Wu of Hsia and his men were doing irrigation work there (Figure 1A). At this time, the Chinese believed that gods lived inside the shells of turtles and tortoises, so the sudden appearance of a tortoise was considered a good omen. However, when they looked more closely at the tortoise, they found that the markings on its shell created a perfect magic square:

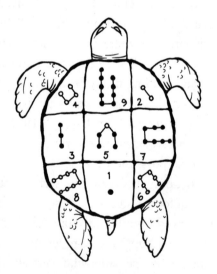

Figure 1A: Tortoise with magic square

$$4 \quad 9 \quad 2$$
$$3 \quad 5 \quad 7$$
$$8 \quad 1 \quad 6$$

Every horizontal, vertical, and diagonal row added up to the number fifteen. This was considered so remarkable that Wu summoned a group of wise men, who studied the phenomenon for a long while. Eventually, they came up with the basics of not only feng shui, but also the I Ching, Chinese astrology, and Chinese numerology.[3]

Partly because of this discovery, Wu went on to become the first emperor in Chinese pre-history. Because it happened so long ago, no one knows if the story is true or not. In fact, it is not even known for certain if Wu ever existed. However, it is a charming story that demonstrates just how old feng shui is.

Feng shui is based on a number of simple principles that we will look at before putting them into practice in your own environment.

Ch'i

Ch'i is the universal life force that is found in all living things. It is created wherever there is beauty, or whenever something is done perfectly. Consequently, both a beautiful garden and an athlete running a mile in under four minutes would be creating ch'i.

The perfect place to live is where there is an abundance of ch'i. This is why the spot favored by the ancient Chinese—with hills behind the home and gently flowing water in front—is ideal. The hills behind protect the house from the cold, harsh north winds that would blow the ch'i away. Gently flowing water creates an abundance of ch'i, which benefits the family. A raging torrent of water would, on the other hand, carry all the ch'i away. Feng shui means "wind and water," but we want gentle breezes and gently moving water to create plenty of ch'i and good feng shui.

Yin and Yang

The ancient Chinese also believed that the universe was in constant motion and that everything could be described in terms of yin or yang. The ancient Taoist symbol of the universe clearly shows this. It is a circle containing two tadpole-like shapes (see Figure 1B). One is black with a white spot inside it. This represents yin. Yang is depicted as a white tadpole with a black spot inside it.

The black spot inside the white, and vice versa, show that neither can exist without the other. Without yin, there could be no yang, and without yang, there would be no yin. The ancients never tried to define yin and yang, but enjoyed coming up with lists of opposites to represent them, such as "night and day". If there was no night, there would be no day. Another would be "front and back." Obviously, if there were no front, there could be no back. Here are some other examples:

Black and white
Tall and short

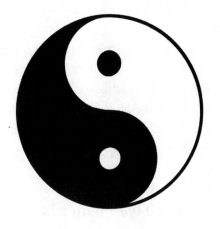

Figure 1B: Yin–Yang symbol

Wet and dry
Hot and cold
Male and female
High and low
Heaven and earth

The words "yin" and "yang" mean the opposite sides of a hill. Yin signifies the shady, northern slopes, while yang represents the sunny, southern side.

All raised areas, such as hills and mountains, are described as being yang, while flat areas are described as being yin. Pagodas were invented to create yang energy in places that were too flat, or too yin.

We want to create a balance of yin and yang in our lives. The ideal place for the Chinese to live contained both yang (the hills behind) and yin (the flat land and the gently moving water in front).

Yin and yang do not sit quietly together. Each is constantly striving to overpower the other. Consequently, in springtime, yang increases while yin decreases. In summer, yang reaches its full power, but declines again in fall, and in winter yin is far more powerful than yang. This cycle carries on ceaselessly from year to year.

The Five Elements

There are five elements in feng shui and symbolically, everything in the universe is composed of these elements. In your Chinese horoscope, you are made up of a mixture of most or all of these five elements. In feng shui, the most important personal element is derived from your year of birth. You can look up your personal element in the Appendix (see page 129).

The five elements are wood, fire, earth, metal, and water, and they can be arranged in a number of ways.

In the Cycle of Production (Figure 1C) each element helps and nurtures the element on either side of it. For instance wood burns, creating fire. Fire produces ashes, which create Earth. From the Earth we derive Metal. Metal symbolically liquefies, creating Water. Water nurtures and produces Wood.

Burning wood
creates fire.

Fire leaves earth.

Wood

Earth

Fire

Water nurtures wood.

Earth creates metal.

Water

Metal

Metal
liquifies.

Figure 1C: The Cycle of Production of the Five Elements

The Cycle of Destruction does the opposite (Figure 1D, next page). Fire melts Metal. Metal chops Wood. Wood drains from the Earth. Earth dams and blocks Water. Water puts out Fire.

Wood

Wood is a creative, sociable, and charming element. If you have a large amount of Wood in your makeup, you will contain these attributes and will have the potential to express yourself creatively in some way. Wood can also be represented by the color green. In the home, Wood can be represented by potted plants and freshly cut flowers.

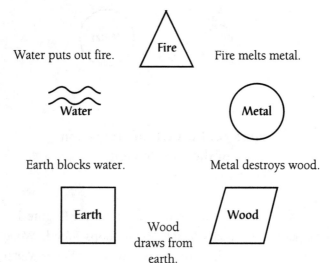

Figure 1D: The Cycle of Destruction of the Five Elements

Fire

Fire is an enthusiastic, active element. It has leadership qualities. However, although Fire can nurture and warm, it can also burn and destroy. Consequently, it needs to be treated with caution. In the home, Fire can be represented by a fire or candles. This is not always convenient. Fortunately, Fire can also be represented by anything that is red in color.

Earth

Earth is stable, reliable, patient, and methodical. It can also be stubborn and demanding. It is related to real estate, legacies, and results obtained through patience and hard work. Earth can be represented by the color yellow. In the home, anything that is made of pottery or ceramics can represent the Earth element.

Metal

Metal is related to business, money, and success. Although it often signifies material success, Metal can also be fashioned into a sword or knife and be destructive. Metal can be represented by white, gold, and other metallic colors. In the home, anything metallic can be used to represent Metal. Ideally, this should be an attractive object made from a precious or semi-precious metal.

Water

Water is related to travel, learning, and communication. Water can be both nurturing and destructive, as in gentle rain and a torrential hurricane. In the home, an aquarium or indoor fountain can be used to represent the Water element. Water can also be represented by anything that is black or blue in color.

We want our personal element to be present in our environment. We also should have in our environment the element that immediately precedes ours in the Cycle of Production, as this element helps to create our own personal element.

Problems can arise, of course, when more than one person is living in the house. In the past, the personal elements of the man of the house always took precedence. Nowadays, it is usually the element of the person who brings the most money into the home.

In practice, the element of the head of the household is used in the main rooms, and the elements of the other members of the family are used in the rooms that they use most.

Ideally, your partner will belong to an element that is compatible with your element in the Cycle of Production. If the two elements are next to each other in the Cycle of Destruction, you will need to use a neutralizing element to eliminate the potential difficulties.

We use the Cycle of Reduction for this. This places the elements in the same order as the Cycle of Production, but it is read counter-clockwise. Consequently, Wood draws from Water. Water corrodes Metal. Metal is created from the Earth. Earth can put out Fire. Fire burns Wood.

Let us say, for example, that you belong to the Metal element and your partner belongs to Wood. These two elements are next to each other in the Cycle of Destruction. This has the potential for trouble, but we can neutralize the harmful effects by including items from the Water element in the home, as Water comes between Metal and Wood in the Cycle of Reduction. An aquarium or small fountain would make an ideal remedy in this instance.

Here is another example. You belong to the Fire element and your partner belongs to Water. A good remedy would be to have something from the Wood element in the house, as Wood comes between Fire and Water in the Cycle of Reduction. In this instance, some potted plants or fresh flowers would make a good remedy.

By doing this, we can resolve potential problems before they begin. It is hard to be happy when you are surrounded by problems. Fortunately, feng shui allows you to live in harmony with all living things (including partners) and has a remedy for almost every problem.

Shars

Shars, frequently referred to as "poison arrows," are straight lines and angles that have the potential for bad luck and misfortune. It does not mean that something bad *will* happen. It simply means that the *potential* for disaster is present.

In ancient China they believed that ghosts could travel only in straight lines. That is why you often see pictures of bridges that zig-zag across ornamental lakes. This is to prevent the ghosts from traveling across them.

Shars can be created in a number of ways. Any straight lines heading directly towards your house are shars. If your house, for instance, is situated at the end of a T-junction, you will have a road heading directly towards your home, creating a major shar. Other common shars are caused by power lines and the roof lines of neighboring houses.

Other shars are caused by angles that, in effect, create an arrow that points towards you. A corner of a neighboring house could create a shar if it sits at an angle to your home.

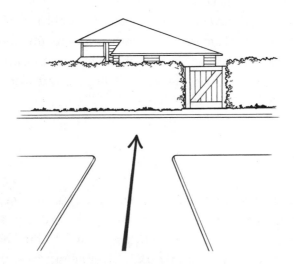

Figure 1E: Concealing a shar

All shars contain the potential for danger. The very worst shars are those that are directed towards your front door.

Fortunately, shars cease to exist if you cannot see them. Consequently a wall, fence, or hedge could be used to eliminate the shar caused by a road heading directly toward you (Figure 1E).

Sometimes a shar cannot be eliminated in this way. Fortunately, there is a remedy for virtually everything in feng shui. A small mirror, known as a pa-kua mirror, can be used to send the shar back to where it came from. A pa-kua mirror is an eight-sided piece of wood, with a small, round mirror in the center. Around the mirror are placed the eight trigrams from the I Ching (Figure 1F).

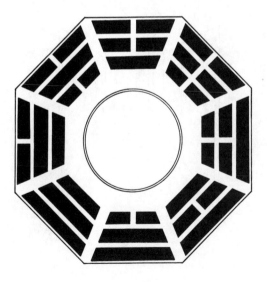

Figure 1F: Pa-kua mirror with trigrams

Mirrors are considered to be yin, or passive. However, when trigrams are placed around them, they become yang, and aggressive. This mirror can be placed above the front door. It symbolically catches the shar in the mirror and sends it back to where it came from.

Pa-kua mirrors should only be used outside the house. They come in three different types. Pa-kua mirrors that contain a flat mirror reflect the shar back where it came from. Pa-kua mirrors that contain a concave mirror absorb the harmful energies. The most dangerous types of pa-kua mirrors contain convex mirrors that reflect the shar off in all directions. These, in particular, should never be used without first consulting an experienced feng shui practitioner.

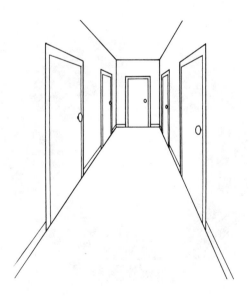

Figure 1G: Long, straight hallway as shar

You can have shars inside your own property, and even inside your home. A straight path leading from the sidewalk to your front door is, in effect, a poison arrow. A long, straight hallway inside your home constitutes a shar (Figure 1G), also. An L-shaped room has a shar created by the two walls that form an angle pointing across the room.

Exposed beams also create shars. Although they may look attractive, they are, in effect, overhead shars that can be oppressive to anyone spending much time directly below them. Make sure that chairs or couches are not placed directly under overhead beams. Check your work environment, also. You are likely to suffer from headaches if you work directly under an overhead beam for long periods of time.

Remedies

In feng shui there is a remedy for virtually every problem. (The two exceptions are water flowing beneath your home and high-voltage power lines immediately overhead.)

Bright lights are extremely beneficial—they make your home feel warm and welcoming. Lights also attract ch'i and can be used to encourage the ch'i to any part of the house you wish.

It is important that the main entrance to your home is well-lit, as this is where most of the ch'i comes in. If your guests find it hard to locate the front door, the ch'i will also.

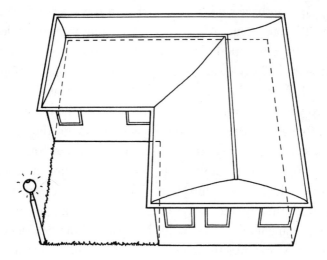

Figure 1H: Lamp used to "square off" L-shape

Lights can also be used to balance irregularly shaped rooms. In Taiwan, outside lamps are used to symbolically "square off" L-shaped homes (Figure 1H).

All light is beneficial, but chandeliers are particularly useful as they reflect the ch'i in all directions. Crystals serve the same purpose on a smaller scale, and make useful remedies.

Mirrors also make effective remedies. They can reflect pleasing views from outside, make small rooms appear larger, and reflect light into dark or gloomy areas. In feng shui, it is important to be able to see the door to the bedroom while in bed without turning your head more than ninety degrees. If, for some reason, this is not possible, a mirror can be used to allow you to see the entrance.

It is also believed that the quality of the meal will be affected if the cook is not able to see the entrance to the kitchen while cooking. A mirror can be placed beside the stove, if necessary, to allow the cook to see a doorway that is behind him or her.

Incidentally in China, mirrors are often placed around the stove to symbolically "double" the amount of food being prepared, representing abundance. For the same reason, mirrors are frequently used in the dining room to double the amount of food on the table.

Speaking generally, mirrors should be as large as possible. This is because small mirrors symbolically "cut off" people's heads and feet.

Plants also make effective feng shui remedies. They create ch'i and symbolize growth and life. Naturally, they need to be healthy. Dead and dying plants create negative ch'i, and should be replaced as quickly as possible. Artificial plants work well, also, but they need to be dusted and kept clean. Dried flowers are not suitable, though, as all the water has been removed from them.

Plants can also be used to conceal and eliminate shars. The sharp corner of a desk, for instance, could be concealed by an attractive potted plant.

Outdoors, plants are probably the most effective remedy of all. Trees can be grown behind the house to provide symbolic protection for the occupants, and real protection from strong winds and noise. They can also be used to eliminate shars coming from outside the property. Evergreen trees are best for this purpose. Trees can also become shars. If they are planted too close to the house they may prevent sunlight from entering, and during the winter months, the branches of trees that lose their leaves could become shars.

Wind chimes and mobiles make attractive feng shui remedies. Movement and sound can revitalize areas that need to be activated. It is possible to obtain wind chimes that relate to your personal element as they are available in a wide variety of materials. Alternatively, you can use metal wind chimes that are painted the correct color to represent your personal element. The pleasing sounds that wind chimes produce remind you that the ch'i is flowing.

It is important that your wind chimes are made of hollow cylinders, as these allow the ch'i to flow up inside them. Other hollow objects, such as flutes, can also be used as a feng shui remedy. Flutes are a common remedy for overhead beams (see page 81 for more information on remedies).

Live animals also create and encourage ch'i. It is rare to find a home in the East that does not contain either a small bird or an aquarium. Water symbolizes money and fish represent forward progress. Together they create a silent affirmation that symbolizes prosperity. Ideally, the fish tank should be large enough to hold nine fish: eight gold fish and one black fish. The gold fish symbolize prosperity and the black one represents protection.

Moving water also provides protection and attracts beneficial ch'i. Small indoor fountains have become popular in recent years, allowing the good ch'i that they provide to be produced indoors and out.

Outdoor fountains and ponds almost always create good feng shui. Naturally, the water must be clean and fresh.

Stagnant, foul-smelling water creates negative ch'i.

Kidney-shaped swimming pools also provide protection if they appear to envelop the house.

Heavy or large objects can be used as a feng shui remedy. This is especially the case where the environment is too yin (too flat). They can also be used to balance a room where most of the furniture is on one side, creating imbalance.

Colors are frequently used as a feng shui remedy. The best way to use color as a remedy is to look at the personal elements of the people involved, and use either the colors that relate to their elements or the color of the element that precedes their element in the Cycle of Production.

The Principles of Successful Living

The Chinese have a saying that lists the five basic principles of successful living. It also clearly demonstrates how important feng shui is in their lives. "First comes destiny, and then comes luck. Third comes feng shui, which is followed by philanthropy and education."

Destiny is determined by our horoscope, and it clearly reveals our strengths, weaknesses, and potential. We cannot avoid destiny. Some people are born to wealthy parents and are given every possible opportunity. Yet, without a strong horoscope, they will not achieve anything. Other people are born in much more modest circumstances. Perhaps their parents cannot afford to feed or educate them. However, if someone like this has a strong horoscope, he or she will rise above these limitations and ultimately become successful.

Second comes luck. The Chinese believe that we can improve our luck by working on the other four principles. This also relates to positive thinking. If we expect good things to happen, they are more likely to occur. The same thing applies if we remain negative and fearful, because we attract to us whatever we think about.

Third comes feng shui. By using the principles of feng shui we can live in harmony with the world and everyone in it. By doing this, we automatically improve the quality of our own lives.

Fourth comes philanthropy. We should give without expecting any reward. This relates to karma. If we do good things for others, sooner or later, we will receive a reward in the form of good things happening to us. Naturally, if we hurt others, sooner or later, we will be made to pay for what we have done.

Finally, comes education. This should be a lifelong process, to enable us to keep up-to-date with what is happening in the world around us.

In many ways, these five principles are also a recipe for happiness. If we make the most of our potential, keep a positive outlook, live in harmony with the world, help other people, and keep on learning, we are bound to be happy.

There is another famous saying in China: "Happiness is a river. It may surround you, but you have to keep swimming." The message is that persistence is also required. Nothing worthwhile happens without a great deal of hard work. If we use our destiny, luck, feng shui, philanthropy, education, and add persistence, we are bound to be successful, fulfilled, and happy.

2

Feng Shui in the Home

Our homes should be places where we can be completely ourselves. We should be able to relax here and forget all the cares and problems of the outside world. Consequently, many of our happiest moments are likely to be spent in our homes.

Using feng shui, we can also make minor adjustments to different parts of our home to bring more success and happiness into our lives.

After we have lived in it for a while, it is hard to look at our home with fresh eyes. However, it is a good exercise to do this every now and then. You are likely to be amazed at the number of things about your home a stranger would notice, but that go past you every day without your notice.

Start the evaluation from fifty yards down the street. Walk towards your home, checking to see if there are any obvious shars that you can remedy. Look at your driveway. From a feng shui point of view it should curve, rather than be a straight line heading directly towards your home. Beds of flowers on each side of the driveway create beneficial ch'i and act as a partial remedy for a straight driveway (see Figure 2A). Your driveway should not be wider at the house end than it is at the road, as this stifles financial opportunities.

The Front Door

Check to see if your guests can find your front door easily. It should be well-lit and appear welcoming. Most of the ch'i that enters your home comes in through the front door. Consequently, we want it to be as attractive, well-lit, and welcoming as possible.

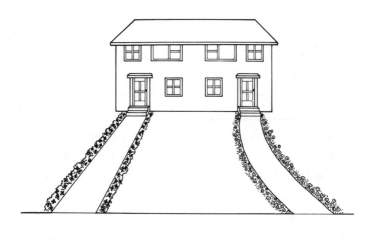

Figure 2A: Flower beds as remedy

Is the front door in proportion to the rest of the house? A too-large front door is believed to create financial problems. Small front doors are inclined to stifle the inhabitants, causing friction, tension, and arguments.

Stand inside your front door and look outside to see if any shars are attacking it. Common ones are likely to be roof lines from neighboring houses, fences, power poles, or extremely large buildings next to your home. Your front door is the single most important factor in feng shui, and any shars should be rectified as quickly as possible. Trees and walls, to shield the shars, make effective remedies here.

When standing at the front door, you should be able to see part of the interior of the house. The entrance foyer should be well-lit and appear welcoming. Dark and gloomy entrances discourage the ch'i from coming in. This ultimately affects the well-being of everyone living in the home. Bright lights and large mirrors make effective remedies in this case.

Large mirrors can be used to make a small entrance foyer seem larger, and screens can be used to make an overly large entrance appear smaller.

The front door should not face a staircase heading upwards, as this confuses the ch'i. It also means that members of the family are likely to come in the front door and head directly to their private rooms, rather than spending time with the other occupants of the house. The remedy for this is to hang a crystal or chandelier from the ceiling midway between the front door and the staircase. This will attract the ch'i upwards and away from the stairs.

The front door should not face the back door, either. In this instance, any ch'i that comes in the front door will immediately race down the hallway and out the back door. If possible, use a screen to conceal the back door. An alternative remedy is to hang a crystal from the ceiling halfway between the front and back doors.

The bathroom should also not be visible from the front door. This is because bathrooms create negative ch'i. The remedy is to keep the bathroom door closed.

If your guests can see inside the kitchen from the front door they will immediately think of food. Immediately after eating your food they will leave. The remedy for this is to somehow conceal the view of the kitchen, if at all possible. A screen could be used to hide the view of the kitchen. If this is not possible, a crystal could be hung from the ceiling halfway between the front door and the kitchen. This encourages the ch'i to flow toward the crystal, rather than the kitchen.

The Living Room

The living room should be a comfortable room where people can relax and enjoy spending time with each other. It should reflect the personalities of the people who live in the house. Consequently, books, photographs, certificates, and anything else that reflects the interests of the occupants should be on view.

It should ideally be square or oblong in shape, and receive sunlight through the windows. If the living room is

Figure 2B: Crowded living room

long and narrow, mirrors should be placed along one of the longer walls to make the room appear better balanced.

The living room should appear spacious. Avoid crowding a small living room with too much furniture (Figure 2B). Space relates to abundance. Consequently, a room filled with furniture and ornaments can constrict the financial well-being of the occupants.

Furniture should reflect the personalities of the occupants and be in proportion to the size of the room. Rounded corners are preferred in feng shui, as square corners send off small shars. Round tables, rugs, lamps and anything else that is oval or circular are considered beneficial, because round shapes symbolize money.

Exposed beams anywhere in the house are bad from a feng shui point of view. This is particularly the case in the living room and bedrooms. Exposed beams affect the smooth flow of ch'i, and people sitting directly under these will gradually feel as if an oppressive weight is on their shoulders. Both of these factors adversely affect the happiness of the family.

The usual remedy for exposed beams is to hang two small bamboo flutes from the center of each beam. Alternatively, an attractive item can be attached to the beam. A far better remedy is to lower the ceiling so that the beams are concealed. Obviously, this remedy is not always a practical one.

The Dining Room

The most important aspect of the dining room is the dining room table. It is important that your guests can get in and out of their seats without being constricted by the walls or other furniture. This is to give the feeling of spaciousness, which relates to abundance. It is important that these abundant feelings are experienced in this room, and this is why mirrors are often used in this room to symbolically double the amount of food on the table. Mirrors are also used here to make a small dining room appear larger.

In the East, the dining room is often part of the living room. This is good, as the larger room creates the feeling of spaciousness. The dining room is also related to money and, consequently, a large dining room is better than a small one for financial growth.

The dining room should be close to the kitchen, but a reasonable distance away from the front door. If it is close to the front door, and especially if the front door is visible, your guests will eat their meals and immediately leave.

Round and oval tables are favored as they enable people to talk easily with everyone else. Square and oblong tables should have slightly rounded corners to eliminate any potential shars.

The Bedroom

Good feng shui in the bedroom is extremely important for peace of mind and happiness. As we spend at least a third of our lives in bed, we probably spend more time in this room than anywhere else in the home.

The bedroom should be reasonably private and as far away from the front door as possible. This means that we are well away from any street noise, and symbolically feel more secure.

The placement of the bed is one of the most important factors in feng shui. (The other vital factors are the positions of the front door and the stove.) The bed should be placed in such a position that people lying in it can easily see anyone coming in through the bedroom door. Usually, the best position for the bed is near the corner of the room that is diagonally across from the door.

If the doorway is behind the bed, a mirror can be used to enable the person in bed to see who is coming in. However, mirrors should be used with great care in the bedroom. For instance, they should not face the bed as this is believed to put strain and pressure on the relationship. Mirrors in the ceiling work well for short-lived, passionate affairs, but also put a strain on long-term relationships.

The foot of the bed should not face the door. In feng shui, this placement is known as the "coffin position." According to Chinese astrology, people should be buried on an auspicious day determined by their horoscope. As this could be as long as a month after the date of death, the coffins used to be lined up in the courtyards of temples waiting for the correct day to be buried.

The bed should not be under any exposed beams. People sleeping under exposed beams are likely to suffer health problems in the part of the body that is directly below the beam. For instance, if the beam is over the chest area, the person would be likely to experience problems with their chest and lungs. If there is no alternative, it is better for beams to run the length of the bed, rather than across it. However, as it is believed that beams running the length of the bed create marital problems, it is better to lower the ceiling to conceal the beams or place the bed in a position where it is not directly under any beams.

The bed should be in contact with a wall to gain support (Figure 2C). It is best if the headboard of the bed makes contact, but it is fine if one side touches a wall. However, a double bed with one side in contact with the wall means

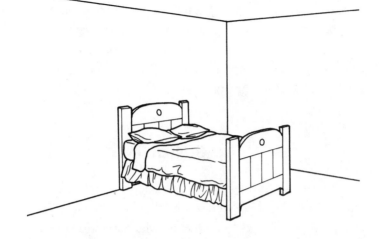

Figure 2C: Position of bed

that the person sleeping in it prefers to sleep alone and does not desire a partner. If you want to encourage a partner, ensure that the headboard of your bed, rather than the side, touches a wall.

The bed should also be in a position where the people sleeping in it will have a pleasant view when they wake up in the morning. A window is perfect, but you need to ensure that the bed does not receive direct sunlight during the day. This is believed to over-activate the bed, making it hard to sleep at night. Ensure that the windows to the bedroom are not affected by outside shars. Heavy drapes can be used to eliminate these if they are present.

The color scheme of the bedroom should harmonize with the colors that relate to the occupants' personal element. In children's bedrooms the correct color is the one that relates to the element that precedes their personal element in the Cycle of Production (see page 7).

The Kitchen

The kitchen has always been considered the most important room in the house from a feng shui point of view. This is because the stove is located here, which is considered to represent the family's wealth.

The kitchen should be well-lit and airy to encourage in the beneficial ch'i. This ch'i is believed to enter freshly cooked meals, providing benefit for the entire family. Naturally, the quality and quantity of food available is important, as it relates directly to the family's prosperity. It is considered a matter of pride to always have a well-stocked refrigerator and cupboard or pantry.

It is important that the person working at the stove is able to see anyone entering the room without turning around. This is because it is believed that the quality of food is affected if the cook gets startled. Naturally, a mirror can be used as a remedy to allow the cook to see anyone coming in, if necessary (Figure 2D).

In fact, it is common to see mirrors around stoves in Chinese restaurants. This is because they symbolically double the amount of food coming out of the oven, giving the potential for greater profits.

Figure 2D: Mirror above stove

As the stove is the seat of the family's wealth, it should be kept clean and in perfect condition. Any problems with the stove create negative ch'i and can affect the family's financial position.

As water symbolizes money, it is important that any drains or pipes are concealed, as it is considered bad feng shui to see your wealth flowing away. Naturally, any leaking taps in the kitchen, or anywhere else for that matter, should be repaired as quickly as possible to prevent the gradual erosion of your wealth.

The kitchen should not be visible from the front door. If it is, your guests will become preoccupied with food as soon as they arrive in your home.

The Toilet

The toilet should be as inconspicuous as possible. In the next chapter we will be discussing the various sectors of a house. A toilet should not be located in the wealth, fame, or career sectors of the home. If it is, your prospects in these areas literally get "flushed" away.

Toilets should be situated on the side of the house. Toilets create negative ch'i, and a centrally situated toilet will send this negative ch'i to every part of the house.

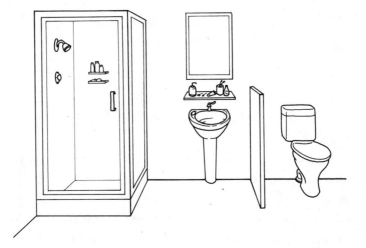

Figure 2E: Half-wall beside toilet

It is better for the toilet to be separate from the bathroom. The Chinese are modest people and like privacy when they are using the toilet. If they happen to be combined in your home, install a half wall to provide a degree of privacy (Figure 2E).

The toilet should not be visible from the front door. The remedy for this situation is to keep the door closed and to have a mirror on the outside of the door to symbolically make the room disappear.

The Bathroom

The toilet and bathroom are both places where water drains away. Consequently, they should be positioned with care. They should also be well-lit, well-ventilated, and always clean. Pastel colors are believed to benefit the family's happiness and well-being.

Mirrors are essential in this room and should be as large as possible. Avoid mirror tiles. They create a "netting effect" that adversely affects the money flow.

In the next chapter we will learn the nine important sectors in your home and how you can enhance them to attract happiness, abundance, and success.

3

The Nine Sectors

*Happiness consists in the attainment of our desires, and in
our having only right desires.*

—St. Augustine

The magic square that Wu of Hsia found in the markings
of a tortoise's shell still play an important part in feng shui
today. Each of the nine sections inside the magic square
relates to a different part of your life. We can improve the
quality of each of these areas of our lives by activating the
part of our home that is indicated by the pa-kua. There
are feng shui remedies and enhancements that can help
you achieve greater success and happiness in each of
these areas.

We start by placing a three-by-three magic square over a
plan of your home. It makes no difference how large or
small your home may be, or if it is a house or an apartment.
If your home is on two or more levels, the magic square is
placed over each level. Naturally, it is easier to do this if your
house is square in shape. If your home is rectangular, the

magic square is also rectangular in shape to accommodate the shape of the house.

L- and T-shaped homes are not as easy to accommodate because when the magic square is placed over their floor plans, part of the square will be outside the area of the house. Fortunately, there is a feng shui remedy for this also.

We need to symbolically complete the home by making it appear square or oblong. We can do this in a number of ways. With an L-shaped house, for instance, we could complete the area that is symbolically missing by erecting a deck. Planting a border of flowers in the place where the house would have extended to if it had been rectangular in shape is another remedy. A large tree can grow to effectively "fill in" the missing area. In Taiwan, the usual remedy is to place an outdoor lamp in the garden in the place that the house would have extended to.

You need not worry if your home is symbolically missing an important area. As well as using the traditional feng shui remedies, we can also activate the area that is missing from the complete home in individual rooms. The same three-by-three magic square can be placed over each individual room in the house, by aligning it with the main entrance to the room.

Once the three-by-three magic square is placed over a plan of the house, we can then interpret it. The side of the house that contains the front door marks the outer edge of three sectors of the magic square: Knowledge, Career, and Mentors. The Wealth sector is as far as you can go diagonally to the left from the front door. The Marriage sector is diagonally to the right. Between them is the Fame sector,

Wealth	Fame	Marriage
Family & Health	Good Luck Center	Children
Knowledge	Career	Mentors & Travel

The main entrance is always on this side of the square

Figure 3A: The Aspirations of the Pa-kua

and in the middle third of the home are the Family, Good Luck and Children sectors (see Figure 3A).

Wealth

Wealth has little or no bearing on personal happiness, but you should activate this area if you want more abundance in your life. Extra money can give you the freedom to do things you may not otherwise be able to achieve. If this will increase your happiness, you need to activate the Wealth sector of your home.

You do this by encouraging more ch'i into this area. This means increasing the amount of light to attract the ch'i in. Proper use of lights, chandeliers, crystals, and mirrors can all accomplish this. You can also use other feng shui enhancements that symbolize money. An aquarium containing eight gold fish and one black fish is a silent affirmation that will remind you of money every time you see it. A small metal container holding a few coins works in the same way. In the East it is common to find these containers in the Wealth sector of people's desks (diagonally to the left from where the occupant sits). Three coins are also often placed under containers holding potted plants.

Metallic objects and round objects also symbolize money and can be used in the sector as a feng shui enhancement to attract wealth to you. Round-leaf potted plants are particularly good, because, as the plant grows, it also symbolizes an increase in wealth.

Fame

Most people do not want to become celebrities who are recognized everywhere they go. However, this sector also relates to our standing and reputation in the community. If you want to become better known or more respected in your neighborhood, you need to activate this part of your home.

You can do this by increasing the amount of light in this sector, and by displaying trophies, awards, and certificates you have earned. An aquarium, especially one that has oxygen aerating it, is extremely good in this position. The bubbles of oxygen symbolize an increase in your reputation. If you want to become famous, you also need to display photographs of yourself, preferably in the company of people who are well-known. If you want to become president of the United States, you should display pictures of previous presidents you particularly admire. If you want to become a famous film star, you should display photographs of successful actors and actresses in this location.

Marriage

Although this location is usually referred to as the Marriage sector, it really relates to all close, intimate relationships. Incidentally, the Chinese believe that whoever sleeps in this part of the house will rule the home. If you have a child's bedroom in this part of your home, you can guess who will be ruling the family!

You should activate this sector if your relationship is not going as well as you would like, or if you are currently on your own and wish to attract a relationship to you.

Naturally, more light is used to attract ch'i into this area. If you wish to improve your current relationship, you also need to have objects in this sector that relate to you and your partner's personal elements. If these two elements are next to each other in the Cycle of Destruction, you should have something in this area that relates to the element that lies between them on the Cycle of Production.

If you want to attract someone into your life, you should also display anything that reminds you of love and romance. For instance, this might be a poster of a couple walking hand in hand along a deserted beach. Whatever it is, make sure that it does not remind you of previous relationships. Do not display photographs or pictures of past relationships, as they will symbolically prevent new relationships from developing.

Warm colors, such as pink and red can also serve to activate this part of your home.

If the Marriage sector contains a bedroom you are not using, make sure that this spare room contains a double bed, and also ensure that you sleep in it every now and then. This bed should be accessible from both sides. A single bed symbolically sends out the message that you do not want a partner, and a double bed that is never used sends out a message of emptiness and loneliness.

Family

Family means our immediate family, of course, but also relates to other people you are close to, such as good friends. If you are having problems with family members, or if you want to attract more friends into your life, you need to activate this area of the house. To do this, you should increase the amount of light, of course, to increase the amount of ch'i flowing into this part of your home. You should also have potted plants, photographs of family members, and objects given to you by relatives and friends.

This area also relates to health. If anyone in the family suffers from a health problem, you should activate this area by using something from the element that precedes this person's personal element in the Cycle of Production.

This is a good location for an aquarium, and for pictures that depict rivers, streams, waterfalls, or lakes.

Good Luck or Spiritual Center

This is an important part of the house as it has the power to influence any of the other sectors. Ideally, every member of the household should use whatever room or rooms occupy this part of the house. Consequently, the dining or living rooms would be ideal here.

This is the worst location for a bathroom or toilet because the negative ch'i they create affects every part of the house.

Children

This area should be activated if you are having problems with your children, or if you want to have children. If you already have children, you should have objects in this sector that relate to the element that precedes theirs in the Cycle of Production. This is a good place to display family photographs and creative items that have been made by members of the family. Any trophies or certificates that have been awarded at school should also be displayed here.

If you want children, this area can be activated by increasing the amount of light, displaying ornaments of small children, or anything else that reminds you of family life.

This area also relates to creativity, and should be activated if you are doing anything creative. This is a good part of the house to display things that you—or other family members—have made or designed.

Knowledge

This sector relates to learning and is a good place for anything that relates to learning and education, such as books, tapes, computers, and a desk. This area should be activated to help family members pursue their education and grow in knowledge and wisdom. In the East, education is considered to be a lifelong pursuit, and this area is almost invariably activated to encourage that concept.

Career

This area should be activated to help family members progress in their careers. This can be done by increasing the amount of light, by displaying metal objects, and by having something that relates to the personal elements of the family members who are out in the workforce. It is also a good place for anything that reminds you of work and career, such as a telephone, computer, or fax machine.

Mentors

This sector should be activated to encourage helpful people into our lives. They say that when the student is ready, the teacher will arrive. By activating this area, we can speed up the process.

This area is also related to travel. If you wish to travel, you should display in this sector anything that relates to the places you want to visit. Photographs and artifacts are ideal.

These areas are not confined within the walls of your house, but extend indefinitely in each direction. Consequently, if you are seeking wealth, you should search in the direction indicated by the room that is as far as it is possible to go diagonally to the left of your front door. Likewise, if you want to progress in your career, the direction is the one that your front door faces.

In practice, you are unlikely to activate all nine areas at the same time. Start by activating the area that is most important to you right now. You will notice an improvement in this area of your life within a few days. Wait about three weeks before activating any other areas. By doing this you will notice how the benefits continue to grow and enhance your life. Then make another change and observe what happens in that area for a few weeks, before making any further changes.

4

Money

It's good to have money and the things that money can buy, but it's good, too, to check up once in a while and make sure that you haven't lost the things that money can't buy.

—George Horace Lorimer

Just recently I watched a television program about a formerly wealthy property developer who had lost all his money and ended up living in the same small cottage where he had begun his empire. In the process, this man discovered that happiness has nothing whatsoever to do with money. He found that he was happier in his small cottage than he had ever been in his luxury apartment.

You may ask why a chapter on this subject is included in this book if money has no bearing on happiness. There are many reasons. Feng shui is extremely good at attracting wealth and abundance. In fact, at my lectures, I usually get asked more questions about money than I do on other aspects of feng shui. Most people believe that if they had more money they would be happier. I am not convinced that this is the case, but if you feel that more money would increase your happiness, you will benefit from following the ideas in this chapter.

The Chinese believe that they have to do well in life to make their ancestors proud of them, and to provide a good foundation for their descendants. There is a whole branch of feng shui dedicated to the location and positioning of graves, as they believe that this has an enormous bearing on the happiness and prosperity of the family. A well-sited grave is believed to provide fame, honor, happiness, longevity, and prosperity for many generations.

The astonishing success of Sun Yat-Sen is attributed to the placement of his mother's grave.[1] In fact, many ambitious people moved their family graves close to that of Sun Yat-Sen's mother's burial place in an attempt to gain some of the benefits of the excellent feng shui.[2] The success of Chiang Kai-shek was also credited to the placement of his mother's grave. His downfall began when the Communists dug up her grave.[3]

I personally believe that happiness is a mindset. We can decide to be happy no matter what our circumstances are in life. Naturally, if a close relative is terminally ill or we are about to lose our home, it is hard to be happy. But it can be done. If we act in a positive manner we not only help ourselves, but we also raise the spirits of the people close to us.

We have already looked at the Wealth sector of our home. Naturally, this should be activated if we want more money. However, there is much more that we can do if we are ambitious and have a strong desire for more money.

Gently flowing water has always been related to money in feng shui. It creates beneficial ch'i and makes the land around it fertile and fruitful. A home that has a view of gently flowing water has always been considered a magnet that attracts good luck, happiness, and wealth. People have always liked living close to water. A comparison of house prices show that people will happily pay a large premium to have a pleasant view of a river, lake, or sea.

The water element has an effect on everyone, no matter what their personal element is. In the Productive Cycle of the elements, Metal symbolically liquefies and creates Water. Water, in turn, nurtures and creates Wood. These three elements are next to each other in the Cycle of Production and they harmonize well. As a result, people born under Metal, Water, and Wood can benefit greatly from the presence of Water in their homes.

You may feel that people born under the Fire and Earth elements miss out on the prosperity aspects of water as they relate negatively to Water on the Destructive Cycle of Elements. This is not necessarily the case. Earth can dam and block Water, as it does in the Cycle of Destruction. However, Water can also nourish Earth and make it fertile. Water puts out Fire in the Cycle of Destruction, but Fire can also heat Water and create steam. Consequently, no matter what your personal element is, you can use Water to bring prosperity into your life.

Gently flowing water creates wealth. However, a raging torrent can do the opposite. It can carry away the beneficial ch'i, leaving havoc and destruction in its wake. This situation can cause people to lose everything. Stagnant or polluted water can cause major health problems, as well as negative ch'i. Consequently, water has to be used carefully.

For instance, many people consider living close to the ocean to be good from a feng shui point of view. Usually, it is. You are extremely fortunate if your home provides a pleasant view of natural, clean, gently flowing water. However, if your home is close to the water's edge and you are constantly exposed to large waves pounding on the beach, you will receive an abundance of negative ch'i. In this situation there is also likely to be a great deal of wind, which would carry away any positive ch'i.

A large building on the seashore, such as a condominium development, will attract better ch'i than a small house, which will sometimes appear to be overwhelmed by the limitless water of the sea or ocean. A large swimming pool can have the same effect when placed next to a small house. However, a small house on the seashore can gain support from nearby houses, softening the potential negative effects.

The best water to have is naturally occurring water, such as a stream, river, lake, harbor, or ocean. Ideally, this water will be in front of the home as this represents financial opportunities that we are able to use. If the water flows behind the house it indicates financial opportunities that we are able to see, but unable to seize. It is often a good idea to erect a wall to conceal a stream or river flowing behind your home, as this effectively removes the frustration that could otherwise result. This is exactly the same as erecting a wall to hide a shar. If you cannot see it, it ceases to exist.

We do not want a stream or river to appear to be heading directly towards our home, as this creates a shar, or poison arrow, that has the potential for harm. Ideally, water that flows past the front of our home should appear to meander, rather than flow in a straight line.

Neither do we want a stream or river to dry up in the summer months, as this means the money flow will also disappear.

The water should be clean and gently moving. Water that is dirty, polluted, foul-smelling, or stagnant creates negative ch'i that can cause financial loss. Sometimes it is possible to purify the water and, if this is done, the financial benefits will increase rapidly.

Obviously, most people are not able to enjoy a pleasant view of naturally flowing water from their front windows. However, they can still enjoy the financial benefits of water in their lives by installing a fountain, pond, swimming pool, or waterfall in their front gardens. This can be just as auspicious as naturally flowing water, and creates an equally large amount of ch'i and wealth.

Naturally, any artificial source of water should be aesthetically pleasing and in proportion to the size of the house.

Fountain

A fountain placed in your front garden and visible from the front door creates an abundance of beneficial ch'i as well as encouraging wealth. There are a large variety of fountains available nowadays, and you should choose one that looks attractive from both the front door and the road. The fountain should be at least thirty feet away from the front door. Remember to turn it on every day to keep the money flowing in. A fountain that is not turned on is like a dried-up river.

Acquaintances of mine installed a fountain in a new home they bought when they moved to New Zealand from Hong Kong. However, they turned it on only when visitors came to the door. As they knew very few people when they first arrived, the fountain was hardly ever turned on, and their fortunes suffered until they got into the habit of turning the fountain on every day.

Fish Pond

A fish pond is extremely good from a number of points of view. It provides water, which creates wealth as well as positive ch'i. It also contains fish, which traditionally mean forward progress, abundance, and great wealth.

In ancient China, the only way to progress was to pass the official examinations. The Chinese observed the fish heading upstream and leaping over waterfalls to get to the breeding grounds. This reminded them of the need to pass exams to get ahead, and fish became motivating forces that symbolized forward progress and ultimate success.

It does not matter which fish you choose, though gold fish provide additional symbolism through their color. *Koi,* or Japanese carp, are another popular choice. This is because the Chinese name for carp (*Lei-Yu*) sounds like "possessing wealth."[4]

Naturally, the pond, the surroundings, and the fish need to be cared for. Dirty water creates negative ch'i, and the potential for financial loss.

Traditionally, the best places for fish ponds are in the north, east, and southeast parts of the garden. A fish pond in the front garden is highly auspicious, but it should never be on the right-hand side of the front door when looking out, as this is believed to cause husbands to stray.

Fish ponds need not be large, but they should be aesthetically pleasing. Do not overstock the pond with fish. Traditionally, nine fish are used: eight gold fish and one black fish. This is because water symbolizes money, gold represents money, and the number eight means money in the near future. The black fish symbolizes protection. If a fish dies it is not necessarily bad luck. It simply means that some disaster has been averted, and you should replace the fish as quickly as possible.

Indoor aquariums should also contain eight gold fish and one black fish. Aquariums are found frequently in homes in Asia, and artists enjoy painting pictures of the nine fish because they know that these works will be easy to sell.

Swimming Pools

Swimming pools are controversial in feng shui. This is because they contain a large amount of water, which can upset the balance of the five elements. Large volumes of water, particularly at the back of the house, are considered potentially dangerous. Consequently, it is better to place a swimming pool to the side or in front of the house.

The best pools are round, oval, or kidney-shaped. Square and rectangular pools create shars from the four corners, which can affect the happiness and well-being of the owners, particularly if the shar is directed at the house.

Small pools are considered better than large ones, because they do not contain as much water. Kidney-shaped pools should appear to embrace the house, rather than face away from it.

Birdbaths

The volume of water does not have to be large, and a well-sited birdbath will encourage financial wealth as well as birds. Naturally, the water needs to be kept clean. The birdbath should be located in a propitious area, ideally where it can be seen and enjoyed from inside the house. A birdbath can be the focal or central point of a garden and create a large amount of beneficial ch'i.

Live animals are good from a feng shui point of view, and the antics of the birds as they use the birdbath provide movement and sound, which help create good feng shui.

Aquariums

Indoor aquariums are extremely popular in Asia and are believed to ensure happiness, success, and wealth, as well as providing protection from disasters. As mentioned earlier, eight gold fish and one black fish are the perfect number to create wealth and protection.

In ancient times most of the population were illiterate and the Chinese devised a large number of "silent affirmations" to motivate and encourage people. Fish are a good example of this. When we see an aquarium, we are likely to think about the pretty fish. However, an Asian looking at the same aquarium will instantly think of money!

Oriental business people use silent affirmations all the time. A beautiful example of calligraphy on the office wall may well say "Profits increase daily." A small metal container with a few coins in it is often found in the Wealth area of a business person's desk. Every time this person sees it he or she receives an instant affirmation of the reason he or she is in business.

Round Objects

Round objects are also related to money, as coins are usually round. Consequently, a round or oval dining room table is more likely to attract wealth than an oblong or square one. Oranges and tangerines are especially good symbols as they are both round and golden in color.

Enjoy Making Money

Another important aspect is that in the East, making money is supposed to be fun. This is why the Chinese smile and laugh a great deal while doing business. They enjoy working hard and they enjoy making money! The busier they are, the more they smile. This, naturally, brings in even more customers, as we all like being served by courteous people who are genuinely pleased to see us. The smile is not artificial. They enjoy working hard, and the harder they work, the happier they are, and the happier they are, the more they smile. There is a great deal of truth to the old saying that a Chinese man without work is a bore. The Chinese enjoy spending time with their work colleagues and customers. They make friends with them, and make money at the same time.

In the East, a pleasant smile is a powerful secret of success. A smile is also excellent feng shui as it smoothes troubled waters and creates happiness and a pleasant environment to work in. The Chinese discovered that it also helps to make money.

5

Health

Health is the soul that animates all the enjoyments of life, which fade and are tasteless without it.

—Sir William Temple

Good health is almost essential for happiness. True, I have met serene and happy people who live with chronic pain, but obviously it is easier to be happy when we are physically well.

Feng shui has a large role to play in creating an environment that encourages good health. Our homes have a vital part to play in the health and happiness of the occupants. Imagine sleeping in a bedroom that was painted bright red or black. Think for a moment about living in a home where the windows were never opened to allow in fresh air. Imagine living in a home where the occupants were so scared of being burglarized that every door inside the house was kept locked at all times. These may sound like exaggerations, but I have seen all of these things, and much more, in homes I have been asked to feng shui. It is not surprising that the health of people living in environments such as these are ultimately affected.

One way of checking your own home for potential health problems is to try to see it with fresh eyes. Simply walk through the house as if you were a prospective buyer. Walk from room to room as if you followed the path of the ch'i as it flows through the house. See if it flows easily and effortlessly throughout the house. Notice if the rooms are well-lit and cheerful. Pause for a minute or two in each room and intuitively pick up the atmosphere. If you stand quietly, the room will talk to you, giving you all the information you need.

There is nothing supernatural or strange about this. We do it all the time. I am sure that you have experienced walking into a room and immediately sensed that something was wrong. All we are doing in this exercise is allowing ourselves to be quiet so that information can come through.

Notice anything that needs to be repaired as you make this assessment. Dripping taps, doors, and windows that stick, and anything else that causes frustration creates negative ch'i. Your happiness, well-being—and even health—will improve once these things in your environment have been repaired.

If anyone in the family has health problems, make sure that this person's bedroom is well-lit and receives plenty of fresh air and sunlight during the day. All of this allows the maximum amount of ch'i to enter the room. Place a live plant in the room to encourage growth and good health. Also place something of the element that precedes the sick person's element in the Cycle of Production in the Family sector of his or her bedroom.

Are you happy with your level of physical fitness? The chances are that you are not, as surveys indicate that most people intend to increase the amount of exercise they do. Of course, good intentions are one thing, acting on them is another.

If you are in good shape physically, you will feel better about yourself and the whole world. You will not only look better, but will be better. Your self-esteem will increase, and you will have more motivation to achieve other goals in your life. You will also have more energy for the activities you enjoy.

Start improving your physical fitness by placing something that relates to the element that precedes your own in the Productive Cycle of the Elements in the Family sector of your home. As you know, this helps create your personal element and will provide you with the motivation to improve your physical fitness.

Decide on whatever it is you are going to do. I find that walking is the most convenient form of exercise for me, but you may prefer to do something completely different. You may decide to join a gym or take an aerobics class. Start slowly. A three-mile walk is almost as good for you as a three-mile jog. However, you will probably not want to start at this level. Take a short walk today, and lengthen it slightly tomorrow. Continue doing this until you are walking for at least twenty minutes without stopping.

Choose your form of exercise carefully. A friend of mine bought a rowing machine to improve her fitness. Her intention was to row for thirty minutes a day while watching television. She quickly discovered that she hated rowing. Also, the machine was bulky and seemed to fill her living room. After a week or two the rowing machine was placed in the spare bedroom and has not been used again. Of course, as it is not being used, it is considered clutter in feng shui. It is often better to rent a machine for a month or two to see if you enjoy that form of exercise before buying the machine.

Many people have told me that their appetites will increase if they start to exercise. This is a myth. Most people find that their food intake actually decreases once they start increasing their level of physical activity.

Physical fitness has an enormous effect on our well-being and happiness. Consequently, we should pay attention to what we eat as well. Probably the single most important thing we can do is to decrease the amount of fat in our diet.

Did you know that it is the amount of carbohydrates you have for breakfast (such as bread or toast) that tells you when you have eaten enough, and when you will be ready for your next meal? The amount of fat you have for breakfast (such as butter or margarine) or the amount of fat you have on your body makes no difference. If you reduce the amount of fat that goes into your system, you will—over a period of time—lose body fat. It takes time, but you *will* lose weight. It is much better to use fatty products for taste, rather than bulk. For example, use a small amount of cheese in a sandwich for flavor, rather than a large slice.

Look after your physical body. Most of us pay more attention to the needs of our automobiles than we do to the body we live in. If something is wrong, see your doctor. Have regular checkups. If you are a smoker, determine to give it up, for your health's sake.

Any time spent exercising and looking after your body will pay rich rewards in happiness and quality of life. You deserve the best life has to offer. Look after your physical body and it will most certainly look after you.

6

Love and Relationships

The greatest pleasure of life is love.

—Sir William Temple

To be completely happy we need to love and be loved in return. I find it sad to read in the newspapers about the shallow lives of many of our favorite film stars. They might have millions of dollars in the bank, but are about to get divorced for the fifth or sixth time. To my mind they are not nearly as wealthy as a couple who may have little or no material wealth, but are surrounded and loved by family, friends, and neighbors.

The divorce and domestic-abuse statistics are appalling. This is particularly sad when you realize that originally these people loved each other. How can relationships that began with love on both sides end so tragically?

Unfortunately, many people embark on married life with unrealistic expectations. They fail to think of the effect that large mortgages, young children, in-laws, and other stresses can have on their relationships. Of course, many other couples have successful relationships that last forever in spite of similar obstacles. Are these people somehow different from the people whose relationships dissolve?

The answer is both "yes" and "no." The couples who enjoy a relationship that grows and develops over the years work at their relationship. They accept their partners for who they are, and do not waste time trying to change them. They appreciate their partners. They communicate. They listen. They share.

If you are in a relationship that seems to be heading nowhere, you are unlikely to be happy. It is up to you to do something about it if the love has gone stale. If you have no desire to restore the relationship, maybe you should end it now. However, remember that at the beginning you wanted to spend the rest of your life with your partner. All relationships take work, and if you really want yours to survive, it is not too late to do something about it.

It can help your relationship to do something that is surprising and out of character every now and again. It need not be large or expensive. It may be something small, such as bringing flowers home.

A friend of mine was going through a difficult time in his marriage, and I suggested that he do something surprising. He called his wife's employer and secretly arranged for his wife to have an afternoon off. At noon on the appointed day, my friend arrived at his wife's office with a basket of food and a bottle of champagne, and took her for a picnic overlooking a lake. This took place several years ago, and his wife still talks about it. They are still married, and my friend says that they really started communicating with each other that afternoon.

True happiness requires successful relationships with other people. Fortunately, we can use feng shui to enhance all our existing relationships and also attract new relationships into our lives.

In the Aspirations of the Pa-kua (see page 37) we learned that the Marriage sector is diagonally to the right as far as it is possible to go from the front door. This area should be activated to enhance any existing relationships or to attract a new one.

You can rekindle the lost passion by activating the Marriage sector with something from the element that precedes your element in the Productive Cycle of Elements. For instance, if you belong to the Fire element, you should introduce something from the Wood element into this part of your home. You might choose a potted plant or some freshly cut flowers to help reactivate the passion.

Be careful not to overdo this, though. A few years ago I evaluated the home of a couple who were having relationship problems. He belonged to the Fire element and his wife belonged to Metal. In an attempt to improve their relationship, the husband had painted the walls green and filled the room with potted plants. He noticed an improvement in his virility, but his wife became even more distant than she had been before. I suggested that he incorporate much less of the Wood element and replace it with something from the Earth element, as this harmonized with both partners. (Fire creates Earth, and Earth creates Metal.)

The ch'i should flow freely throughout the Marriage sector. This area also needs to be kept free of clutter.

Just recently I conducted an evaluation for a couple and found that the Marriage sector of their home was a dusty storeroom that was seldom used. The windows were kept shut and the door was always closed, ensuring that no ch'i was able to enter. Most of the items stored in this room related to a previous business venture that had failed. The wife confided in me that their marriage had failed as well, and the house was definitely an "unlucky" one for them. I suggested that they clear this room out, redecorate it, and use it on a regular basis. The husband was unenthusiastic about doing this, but they noticed an immediate improvement in their lives as soon as they got rid of the clutter that had been gradually strangling their relationship.

This shows how important it is to allow the beneficial ch'i to flow freely through the Marriage area of your home. There should be sufficient lighting in this part of the house to encourage the ch'i. The room or rooms should appear attractive to encourage feelings of comfort and pleasure. Any beds in this part of the house should be accessible from both sides to encourage romantic relationships.

The Marriage sector applies to all close relationships. They do not necessarily have to be romantic. For instance, if you are in business with a partner, this particular relationship can be enhanced by activating the Marriage sector of your home. You should also activate this area in your business premises.

Most non-romantic relationships are represented by the Family sector of the home. Again, this part of the house should be well-lit and appear welcoming. Any chairs or couches should be used on a regular basis to encourage people to visit.

Loneliness is incredibly common, and is related to despair, illness, depression, and suicide. Yet there is no need to be lonely if you do not want to be. However, you have to make an effort.

All relationships need to be nurtured. There is an old saying, "to have a friend, be a friend."

You have to be prepared to make the first move. A simple comment about the weather or the situation you are both in can open the door to an interesting conversation that may just lead to a friendship.

My first visit to India was a direct result of a friendship I made with an elderly man at a bus stop. We both used to wait at the same bus stop every morning, and for three months neither of us spoke to the other. One morning, I happened to comment that the bus was even later than usual. Over the next several months he told me all about his experiences as a tea planter in India. He turned out to be a fascinating man who ultimately became a friend of my whole family. If I had not made the first contact, we would never have become friends and my life would have been poorer as a result.

Most people are scared to make the first move. It took me three months the first time, but I have improved since then!

Once you have made a friend or two, you have to keep them. You may invite them to your home, or suggest interesting activities that you can do together. Be interested in what they have to say. Friendship is a two-way relationship. Gradually, reveal more of yourself to your friends, and allow them to do the same with you. Help and encourage them when you can, and allow them to help you in return. Be gentle and kind with your friends, and remember to be just as kind and gentle with yourself. Accept your friends as they are, and accept yourself in the same way. You are fine. You are perfect just the way you are now. You can have as many friends as you want if you simply remember to be a friend in return.

The Family location is a good place to communicate with your friends. You might phone them from here, or perhaps write letters or e-mails. This is also a good place to entertain your friends and to display photographs of you and your friends enjoying fun activities.

As your relationships continue to grow and develop, you will also change and become more compassionate and loving. By being a friend to others, your happiness will expand exponentially.

7

Spirituality

Faith is the pencil of the soul that pictures heavenly things.

—T. Burbridge

This may seem an unlikely topic for a book on happiness, but in practice it is not. To be truly happy, we need a faith or philosophy to live by. A faith in something greater than ourselves can enhance our lives and make everything worthwhile.

All faiths have a number of things in common relating to our conduct and how we should live our lives. Concepts about honesty, loving one's fellow man, and doing unto others as you would have them do unto you, provide excellent guidance for getting along with others whether you have a strong faith, or none.

If you belong to an organized religion, become involved with it. Take part in humanitarian activities. Worship with other members of the congregation. By doing this you will enrich your life in many ways. You will be able to help others, you will make good friends, your faith will grow, and your life will become an example for others to follow.

Maybe you do not consider yourself a religious person. All the same, you can gradually create a worthwhile philosophy of life by reading, meditating, and talking with others. You can grow inwardly just as much by doing this.

We need to nurture the spiritual side of our natures just as much as our physical, mental, and social sides. Only when we can see beyond the temporal and open ourselves up for spiritual nourishment can we truly claim to be fully alive.

In feng shui, the middle of your home is called the Spiritual Center. Also, of course, the central part of every room inside the house is also a spiritual center.

The central part of the home is an excellent place for family members to spend time together. Consequently, it is a good location for part of the living room or dining room. It is also an excellent position for sacred space. Joseph Campbell described sacred space as being a place where wonder can be revealed.[1]

The center of your home is the ideal place for a small oasis of peace and calm where you can sit quietly by yourself and restore your soul. Throughout history, people have needed a quiet place to meditate and be in harmony with the universe.

This area can be furnished in any way you wish. I have a comfortable recliner chair that I use. A friend of mine has a Persian prayer rug that he unrolls and sits on when he needs to think and become in tune with the infinite. I like to have photographs of the special people in my life in this part of our home. There is no right or wrong way to set up your sacred space. You may choose something completely different from what I have.

A woman I know sets up a temporary altar in her sacred space and covers it with cheap jewelry. I think this looks garish, but I have never commented on it, because it is right for her.

Another woman I know uses the center of her kitchen as her sacred space. She is a keen flower arranger and her freshly-cut flowers are always placed in the middle of her kitchen for a few minutes before being taken to other rooms for display. "I am in total control here," she told me. "This is my room in the house, and consequently my sacred space is here."

This is true. Your sacred space does not have to be in the center of your home. It can be anywhere, indoors or out.

I have a personal oracle tree on farmland near where I live, and I sit under it whenever I need to meditate or think things through. The oracle tree comes from the druidic tradition, and consists basically of a contract you make with your oracle tree. You agree to look after the tree and its immediate surroundings and it, in turn, will look after you.[2]

An elderly man I know had his personal sacred space at work. At lunchtime every day he would close his office door and meditate at a small altar for several minutes. His altar was organized in such a way that no one was aware of what it was.[3] He attributed his business success to the fact that for a short time every day he was able to let go of all his problems and simply become in tune with the universe.

You may wish to perform a ceremony of some sort in your sacred space. You can do this on your own or with other members of the household. I know several couples who do this together, and also know other people who perform a ceremony on their own, without their partner's knowledge. Whatever you do is entirely up to you. You should allow a few minutes to relax and remove yourself from the stresses and strains of the everyday world. I find it helpful to roll my shoulders a number of times to release the tension that gathers there. I use a self-hypnosis technique to completely relax. Repeating a mantra or concentrating on your breathing can help you achieve the same result.

Once you are completely relaxed you might want to say a prayer, and give thanks or ask for guidance, forgiveness, or anything else that you are concerned with. You may choose a familiar prayer that you know by heart, or you may simply let the words come to you. You may prefer to sit quietly and let your thoughts roam as they wish.

When you are ready to finish, quietly give thanks, take a few deep breaths, and open your eyes.

Many people have told me that they do not have time for something like this. However, they find time for all sorts of things that are much less beneficial to them. I find that I have so much more energy after spending time in my sacred space that I can achieve much more than I would have otherwise. Consequently, these sessions save me time, and also allow me to contact my spiritual side.

Activating the Spiritual Center of your home will impact every area of your life. You will find yourself becoming more accepting, compassionate, gentle, and loving. You will become less rigid in outlook, more forgiving, and more holy.

As the spiritual side of your being becomes more and more apparent, your happiness will grow and expand.

8

Feng Shui Remedies

The habit of being happy enables one to be freed, or largely freed, from the domination of outward conditions.

—Robert Louis Stevenson

One of the most useful aspects of feng shui is that there is a remedy for virtually everything. If there is any aspect of your life that you are not happy with, you can improve it by using feng shui.

Remedies, sometimes referred to as *cures,* can be divided into two types. Remedies can be used to enhance an area that has nothing intrinsically wrong with it. An example of this is to increase the amount of light in a certain area to encourage more ch'i into that part of the house. They can also be used to remedy, or cure, a particular problem. The use of a pa-kua mirror to reflect back a shar is an example of this.

Some remedies, such as the pa-kua mirror, are used only out of doors. Crystals are used inside the house, but other remedies can be used both inside and out.

Outdoor Remedies

Plants

Trees, shrubs, and hedges can all be used to conceal shars that affect your home. Plants can also conceal unpleasant views, provide protection from harsh winds, and help eliminate excessive noise. They can also be used to create more yang energy if the landscape is completely flat (yin).

In the past, groves of trees were planted behind homes, and even behind entire villages, to provide symbolic protection. It is still possible to see these feng shui woods protecting remote villages in the New Territories of Hong Kong. They are usually crescent-shaped groves of native trees, although bamboo is also frequently used.[1]

Trees should be allowed to grow naturally. Consequently, it is important to determine how high a certain plant will grow before planting it. Trees should not be planted too close to the house, as they can ultimately block out the sun and prevent valuable ch'i from entering the home.

Your plants should be healthy. Dying or rotting plants create negative ch'i and should be removed as quickly as possible.

All flowers are good and create an abundance of ch'i. However, five flowers traditionally were considered better than others because they have a special feng shui significance. These special flowers are: peonies, chrysanthemums, white magnolias, orchids, and lotuses.

The peony is the most fortunate of these flowers and represents wealth, honor, and love. When it blossoms it symbolizes great fortune. During the T'ang Dynasty, the peony was known as the "king of flowers" and symbolized a rich and happy person.[2]

The chrysanthemum symbolizes happiness and laughter. This is a good flower to have indoors as well as out, as it symbolizes a life of comfort and ease. Chrysanthemums also symbolize autumn. (Bamboo symbolizes summer; plum-blossoms, winter; and epidendrums, spring.)

Peonies and chrysanthemums are found everywhere during the Chinese New Year celebrations.

White magnolias and orchids symbolize good taste, sweetness, and femininity.

The lotus has always been considered a sacred flower by the Buddhists, and symbolizes purity. This is because it rises out of muddy water and sits triumphantly on the surface. Inside the home the lotus represents peace, tranquillity, creativity, and spirituality. White and red varieties of the lotus can be found in China, and they are frequently depicted in paintings where they are often depicted as a throne or carriage for a god or goddess.

Geraniums are also good flowers to have in your garden. Red ones are believed to attract prosperity, while white ones give peace of mind and pleasant dreams.

Holly attracts money and works best if planted in the southeast. Anything round symbolizes money. The common dandelion is a good example and is also believed to keep family members in good health.

Jasmine symbolizes friendship and affection. Cornflowers are also good for stimulating and maintaining good relationships.

Daffodils symbolize generosity, open-mindedness and communication. However, they should be used sparingly, as too many can dissipate your energies.

Roses are extremely beneficial, especially when you have an odd number of them in your garden.

Tulips, especially red ones, symbolize love and romance.

All plants are good from a feng shui point of view. I have included much more information on plants in my book *Feng Shui in the Garden.*[3]

Water

Water can also be used as an effective outdoor remedy. Most large cities are too yang, and a pond or waterfall can provide the necessary yin balance to create harmony, contentment, and happiness. These benefits can be enhanced further with attractive landscaping, as plants create good luck.

Naturally, the water needs to be kept clean, because dirty, stagnant or foul-smelling water creates negative ch'i.

Fish ponds are highly beneficial. Not only do they provide water, but the fish symbolize wealth and abundance, as well as upward progress.

Carp are extremely popular in China. In Chinese, the name "carp" sounds like "have wealth," which is highly auspicious. Carp are also silent affirmations. Every March, the carp struggle their way across rapids and up waterfalls in the Yellow River to reach their breeding grounds. The courage and endurance of these fish is taught to children to show them that they must have these qualities to succeed in life.

Fountains are excellent in creating ch'i, and symbolize the movement of money. Consequently, they are often found outside the main entrances of buildings that are dedicated to making money. A fountain outside the front door of your home will create ch'i and increase your wealth.

Lights

Outdoor lights are an extremely useful feng shui remedy for buildings and land that are irregular in shape. A lamp can be used to symbolically fill in the empty area formed by an L-shaped house. If the piece of land is L-shaped, the remedy is to have a lamp at the corner that faces the "missing" piece of land.

A light behind the house makes an effective remedy for other irregular shaped pieces of land.

Lights can also be used to provide balance in situations where the house has been built on one side of the plot.

Pa-kua Mirror

A pa-kua mirror can be used to reflect shars back to where they came from. Mirrors are considered yin, and passive, but pa-kua mirrors are yang, and aggressive. Consequently, they should be used with caution. See if it is possible to remedy the situation with other methods first, and use the pa-kua mirror as a last resort.

Indoor Remedies

Lights

Anything that captures or reflects light can be used as a remedy. Light fittings, crystal objects, and mirrors are all effective remedies. They can be used to attract ch'i into dark corners, or any area that we wish to activate.

Mirrors can be used to reflect attractive views from the outdoors inside. If you have a pleasant view of water or countryside, you can use a mirror to bring this good fortune inside your home, providing you with an abundance of beneficial ch'i.

Mirrors symbolically double what they see, and can be used to make small rooms appear larger or to reflect the amount of food on the dining room table, enhancing feelings of abundance.

Mirrors can also be used to remedy L-shaped rooms. Mirrors on the two protruding walls eliminate the shar, by symbolically making the angle disappear.

Generally speaking, mirrors should be as large as possible. Small mirrors symbolically cut off heads and feet. However, all mirrors are beneficial and you cannot have too many of them in your home.

Crystals are extremely useful as they attract the ch'i and then send it out again in every direction. A crystal chandelier is a veritable magnet for the ch'i. Crystal vases, paperweights and other decorative objects made of crystal work in exactly the same way, and are extremely beneficial in creating harmony, contentment, and happiness.

Plants

Plants are just as useful indoors as they are outdoors. Naturally, they should be well cared for and appear strong and healthy. Potted plants and freshly cut flowers create an abundance of ch'i, and a more pleasant environment.

Good quality artificial plants are also effective, but they must be kept dusted and clean. Dried flowers, of course, should be avoided as they have had all the water drained from them. This creates strong negative ch'i.

As well as encouraging ch'i, plants symbolize life, growth, and upward progress.

Plants can be used to remove potential shars created by sharp angles, square columns, and long hallways.

Freshly-cut flowers can be used to activate any sector of the home that you wish. They are particularly effective in the Marriage, Family, and Mentors areas.

Water and Fish

Water is highly positive in feng shui. However, you need to ensure that you do not use too much water, particularly if you belong to the Fire element. Small indoor fountains have become extremely popular and provide an excellent source of ch'i. As well as creating ch'i, they look attractive and provide movement.

Aquariums are also beneficial as they contain both water and fish. Fish, like plants, are alive and symbolize growth, forward progress, wealth, and abundance. It is common in Asia to find ponds containing turtles and gold fish in temple

gardens. The turtles symbolize longevity and the fish represent wealth. Statues of fish are also sometimes seen on the
roofs of temples. They are there to ward off fire. They also
symbolize freedom from restrictions, and are considered a
holy emblem in Buddhism.[4]

The fish need not be alive to symbolize prosperity. A
painting depicting fish or a fish ornament provide the same
benefits. I have a ceramic fish in my office.

As mentioned earlier, eight gold fish and one black fish
are the perfect number to have. However, two fish symbolize marital harmony and are often used to bless a newly
married couple.

Sounds

Wind chimes and bells make effective remedies. Wind
chimes have the advantage of being available in a variety of
materials, and can also be painted to match anyone's personal element. The essential quality is that the rods be hollow to allow the ch'i to rise inside them.

Whenever they are caught by the breeze, a pleasant sound
is heard that reminds people that the ch'i is flowing.

Bells are also useful. Naturally, as someone has to tap or
shake them to create a pleasing sound, they are not used as
commonly as wind chimes.

Ceremonial gongs are sometimes found in homes in the
Far East. These are used to symbolize the family's wealth
being passed on from generation to generation. They are
generally kept in the dining room to represent an abun-

dance of food. Bells and gongs are particularly useful for creating sacred space, as their sounds resonate throughout the house.[5]

Bamboo flutes are a common remedy for overhead beams. Two bamboo flutes are hung from each beam. Traditionally they are hung from red ribbon, at an angle to each other, and with the mouthpieces at the bottom. These flutes are not played, of course. However, the sweet, pure sounds of a flute are believed to raise the spirits of anyone who can hear them. It also increases confidence, self-esteem, and makes people feel safe and protected.

As radios and television sets produce pleasing sounds, they can be used as feng shui remedies. However, they need to be used with caution, as they can also create negative ch'i when the sounds are discordant.

Moving Objects

Mobiles, windmills, revolving doors, and fans all come into this category. Mobiles and revolving windmills look attractive and move gently in the breeze. They are sometimes used as an alternative to wind chimes. This is because some feng shui practitioners do not like wind chimes indoors and prefer to have them outside. I have always enjoyed having wind chimes inside my home and find them extremely useful.

Revolving doors provide a remedy for shars created by long hallways and any other straight lines heading directly towards the door.

Fans keep the ch'i moving and prevent it from becoming stale or stagnant. This is particularly important in dispersing odors and in freshening rooms that are seldom used.

Heavy Objects

Heavy objects, such as rocks, statues and large pieces of furniture, are used to balance areas that are too yin, or flat. They can also be used to harmonize a room that may have most of the furniture on one side.

Evaluate the problem area carefully before adding a heavy object. Sometimes you can change the placement of the furniture to achieve balance without adding something large and heavy.

Colors

The colors relating to each of the five elements can be used to create harmony and balance in the home. The main rooms should contain colors that relate to the personal element of the head of the house, while the other rooms should reflect the element of whoever in the household uses them most. Naturally, you should use colors that reflect your personal tastes, and these may not accord with the colors dictated by the Cycle of Production. Fortunately, some small object of the correct color is all that is required to satisfy the needs of the occupant's personal element.

Light colors should be used for ceilings. Dark colors symbolize a cloud hovering over the occupants. This feels oppressive and creates stagnant ch'i.

Red has always been considered a color of good luck. This is why the decor of Chinese restaurants is often red and gold. Red packets containing money are distributed to employees and children during the Lunar New Year.

Gold symbolizes wealth and prosperity.

Green is related to spring, the season of rebirth. Consequently, it symbolizes encouragement and growth.

Black is usually considered a negative color, but it can be an excellent choice, particularly for people from the Water element. Naturally, it needs to be used with care, but striking results can be obtained.

Color choice is a highly personal matter and your aesthetic judgment is more important than the colors that relate to the five elements.

9

Recipes for Happiness

Adversity's sweet milk, philosophy.

—William Shakespeare, *Romeo and Juliet,* Act 3, scene 3

The Chinese have a unique philosophy and view of life. Conditions were extraordinarily difficult for thousands of years and life was a constant struggle just to survive. In fact, life must have seemed pointless, until people started living in harmony with the earth, instead of trying to fight it.

Over thousands of years, a philosophy of life developed. This was based on an acceptance of what life brings. There was no need to strive after wealth or fame; life could be extraordinarily rich if one approached it in a detached, accepting manner. If you did this, you could be extremely happy, no matter what happened to you.

The two most famous philosophers in Chinese history were Lao-tzu and Confucius. It is remarkable that three of the greatest thinkers who ever lived were born within twenty years of each other. Lao-tzu was born about 570

B.C.E., Buddha in 563, and Confucius in 551. Lao-tzu's birthdate is approximate, but he was a contemporary of the others, as there are numerous accounts of a rebuke he gave to Confucius when the younger man came to visit him.

The influence that Lao-tzu and Confucius had on Chinese thought is immeasurable.

Lao-tzu

The Chinese are a pragmatic, practical, down-to-earth people who have produced very few mystics. The most famous was Lao-tzu, who lived some two and a half thousand years ago. He was the author of the *Tao Te Ching* (The Way).[1] Lao-tzu is credited with founding Taoism, which is not strictly correct, as Taoism began well before he was born.[2]

Little is known about Lao-tzu's life. He is believed to have lived to the age of a hundred and sixty. At one time he was curator of the National Library in Luoyang, at that time the capital of the Chou Dynasty.[3]

As an older man he is believed to have met and rebuked a young Confucius for being overly proud and ambitious. Confucius was so impressed with the old sage that he compared him to a dragon that can soar and fly on the winds and clouds.[4]

Originally, the word Tao meant a particular course of action, probably a military one, as the character combines "foot" with "leader."[5] Lao-tzu interpreted tao as being the way, the essence of the universe. In one poem he describes the way as being a void that can never be filled, but out of which everything comes.

Lao-tzu claimed that his teachings were easy to follow and put into practice. However, his choice of language made it difficult for the ordinary people to understand him. Countless interpretations over the centuries have sometimes threatened to hide what was essentially a perfect way of living. All the same, he has been respected and venerated throughout the ages for his ideas and philosophy. The Confucianists considered him a great philosopher, the Taoists considered him divine, and the common people considered him to be "a saint or god."[6]

Lao-tzu had a great deal to say about the art of living, and his book, the *Tao Te Ching,* could almost be considered a recipe for happiness.

Be Humble

Lao-tzu uses the analogy of water to explain this concept. He says that although nothing is softer than water, nothing is better at weakening and wearing down the hard. In other words, the weak can overcome the strong, and the gentle can win over the firm.

Lao-tzu says that a good man is like water. Water nourishes and supports life, but it never tries to take over the high ground. It is content to remain in the low places, because it knows that the great oceans rule over all the streams and rivers purely because they are in the low position.

You should give first, if you want to take. You should humble yourself, by placing yourself below others if you want to be above them. Jesus shared this philosophy and demonstrated it when He washed the feet of His disciples. By putting Himself below them, He was actually demonstrating that He was above them.

Therefore, you should not struggle and strain to progress. You should remain calm and serene, and work diligently until the right moment comes along. You should seize this moment and achieve your goals in an unforced, natural way.

Be Compassionate

Lao-tzu listed three treasures: compassion, frugality, and a lack of interest in being first.

By being compassionate you will be concerned for the well-being of others. This means that you will not forget others in your desire to progress.

When you are frugal you can better use your own resources.

If you have no desire to contest the number one position, you are likely to find yourself there.

Lao-tzu illustrated these concepts by explaining that while people are alive, their bodies are soft and mobile. When they are dead, their bodies become stiff and rigid. Plants are also pliable while alive, but dry and brittle once they are dead.

Consequently, being rigid and immovable is similar to death. By remaining soft and pliable, and being prepared to bend or yield when necessary, you will ultimately succeed.

Lao-tzu describes a good general as one who uses war only when there is no alternative, and stops as soon as his objective has been achieved. He takes no pleasure from the victory, because he does not enjoy killing others. General Norman Schwartzkopf is a good modern-day example of such a person.

Limit Your Desires

Lao-tzu wrote that people who take less will have more. People who desire more will ultimately become obsessed, and their desires will get in their own way. Limitless greed is the ultimate vice. Lao-tzu considered that no disaster was worse than insatiable desires.

If you are content with what you have, it will be sufficient and you will be happy. You enjoy peace of mind when your desires are few.

Step Out of Yourself

When you are too close to your ego, you are inclined to worry and become anxious about external things. Life becomes more harmonious only when you forget yourself. You will enjoy life more once you stop thinking about yourself.

The more you do for others, the more you will have yourself. Once you stop being selfish, your goals will be realized. Only a truly selfless person could successfully govern the world.

Take One Step at a Time

It always pays to handle the smaller difficulties before starting work on the larger ones. If you want to achieve great goals, set a series of smaller ones that will lead you toward your ultimate goal. Perhaps the most famous words of Lao-tzu are: "A journey of a thousand miles begins with one small step."

People who achieve great things do not consider themselves great. They plan what they want to accomplish, and are aware of any difficulties that might occur on the way toward their goal. By doing this, they can deal with any problems before they grow too large to handle.

These people are aware that as we get nearer to our goal, we are more prone to fail. Consequently, they are as careful at the end as they were at the beginning.

Know When to Stop

It is always better to stop before the cup overflows. In other words, stop as soon as the job is done. Do not talk too much, or stay too long.

If you remain patient, unassuming, and content, you will lead a sound life full of happiness.

Lao-tzu, himself, was aware of how hard it was to put all of these precepts into practice.

Confucius

Confucius is best known today for his aphorisms, but he was a dedicated historian, and it was his study of history that enabled him to create his philosophy. His concept of moral and social order is called *li*, a word that is virtually untranslatable in English. In a sense, it symbolizes a perfect world with everything in its correct place. It also symbolizes righteousness, good manners, fairness, and even faith. In China, Confucianism is sometimes referred to as the "religion of *li*."[7] Confucius was known as "The Throneless King,"[8] but was also frequently condemned and ridiculed during his life.

Confucianism is a philosophy that includes personal ethics, empathy, and a deep compassion for others. Confucius believed that by training men to be honest and compassionate the world would be a much happier and more harmonious place. He called these honest and compassionate people "superior men."

Confucius described a superior man by saying that he was a combination of three different types of man: a true man, a wise man, and a brave man. A true man, according to Confucius, has no worries, a wise man has no confusion, and a brave man is afraid of nothing.

His followers felt that this described Confucius himself. However, he felt that he had not succeeded, admitting only that he had tried his best. This was probably because he was never appointed to an important position, and felt he was unappreciated.

However, despite Confucius' lack of success in his lifetime, his legacy is still strong in China today, and contains valuable lessons for all of us. Cooperation and loyalty within the family unit, and a strong social concern benefit everyone and hurt no one.

The Chinese believe that we achieve a form of immortality when we leave the world a better place than it was when we were born. This allows us to leave a "fragrance" behind that will last for one hundred generations. If we care for family and friends, continue learning all the way through life, work hard, and have a strict code of integrity, we will be happy, successful, and lead worthwhile lives.

10

Fortunate and Unfortunate Directions

Happy the man, and happy he alone,
He, who can call today his own;
He who, secure within, can say,
Tomorrow do thy worst, for I have lived today.

—John Dryden's translation of Horace

We all have four positive and four negative directions, determined by our year of birth. If you have traveled in the East you probably noticed how interested the Asians are in gambling. The prosperity direction is one of the favorable directions, and they like to face this direction when gambling. I have seen two gamblers arguing when they both wanted to face the same direction.

The Compass School of feng shui uses the eight trigrams from the I Ching to determine our positive and negative directions. The eight trigrams are comprised of every possible combination of broken and unbroken lines. The unbroken lines represent yang (male) energy. The broken lines are related to yin (female) energy.

There is a simple formula that will tell you which trigram you belong to.

If you are male, subtract the last two digits of your year of birth from 100, and then divide by nine. The answer is ignored; it is the remainder that is important.

For instance, if you are a man who was born in 1957, we subtract 57 from 100, which gives us an answer of 43. We divide 43 by nine, which gives us a remainder of 7 (9 x 4 = 36, with 7 remaining.). His trigram is Tui.

Here is another example, this time for a man born in 1964. 100 - 64 = 36, and 9 x 4 = 36, with no remainder. He is a Li.

The formula for women is slightly different. You begin by subtracting 4 from the last two digits of your year of birth, and then divide the answer by 9. Again, the remainder is what is important.

Here is an example of a woman born in 1944. We subtract 4 from 44, leaving 40. 40 divided by 9 is 4, with a remainder of 4. She, therefore, is a Sun.

We determine which trigram we belong to by using the remainder and referring to this chart:

If the remainder is **one**, the person is a **K'an.**
If the remainder is **two**, the person is a **K'un.**
If the remainder is **three**, the person is a **Chen.**
If the remainder is **four**, the person is a **Sun.**
If the remainder is **five**, the person is a **K'un if male,**
and a **Ken if female.**
If the remainder is **six**, the person is a **Chien.**
If the remainder is **seven**, the person is a **Tui.**

If the remainder is **eight,** the person is a **Ken.**

If the remainder is **no remainder,** the person is a **Li.**

Each of the trigrams has a meaning and relates to a different part of your home.

Chien

CHIEN - The Creative

Chien is made up of three unbroken (yang) lines. It is related to the father of the family and the rooms that he is likely to use, such as the study, den, office or main bedroom. Chien's direction is northwest.

K'un

K'UN - The Receptive

K'un is made up of three broken (yin) lines, and symbolizes the maternal qualities. Consequently, it is related to the mother and the rooms that she would usually occupy, such as the kitchen and sewing room. K'un's direction is southwest.

Chen

CHEN - The Arousing

Chen is made up of two broken (yin) lines above an unbroken (yang) line. It represents the east direction and the eldest son. Consequently, this is a good part of the house for his bedroom.

Sun

SUN - The Gentle

Sun is made up of one broken (yin) line beneath two unbroken (yang) lines. It represents the southeast direction and the eldest daughter. Her bedroom should be located in the southeast part of the house.

K'an

K'AN - The Abysmal

K'an is made up of one unbroken (yang) line between two broken (yin) lines. It represents the north and the middle son. His bedroom should be situated in the north part of the house.

Li

LI - The Clinging

Li is comprised of one broken (yin) line between two unbroken (yang) lines. It represents the south and the middle daughter. The south is a good direction for her bedroom.

Ken

KEN - Keeping Still

Ken is comprised of two broken (yin) lines below an unbroken (yang) line. It represents the northeast and the youngest son. His bedroom should be in the northeast part of the house.

Tui

TUI - The Joyful

Tui consists of two unbroken (yang) lines beneath a broken (yin) line. It represents the west and the youngest daughter. Her bedroom should be in the west part of the house.

East Four and West Four Houses

The trigrams can be divided into two groups: the East Four Houses (Li, K'an, Chen and Sun) and the West Four Houses (Chien, K'un, Ken and Tui). The trigrams in the East Four Houses belong to the Fire, Water, and Wood elements, which as you know from the Productive Cycle of Elements, is a highly compatible grouping. The trigrams in the West Four Houses belong to the elements Earth and Metal, which is also highly harmonious.

You are likely to be happier in a house that belongs to the same grouping that you belong to. For instance, if you are a Tui, you would be happiest in a Tui house. However, you would also be extremely happy living in a Chien, K'un or Ken house, as they all belong to the same grouping (East Four Houses) as you.

The correct home for you is determined by the direction that the back of your house faces. In feng shui, this is known as the direction in which the back "sits." The directions are shown in the following chart:

A LI house sits to the south and faces north.
A K'UN house sits to the southwest and faces northeast.
A TUI house sits to the west and faces east.
A CHIEN house sits to the northwest and faces southeast.
A K'AN house sits to the north and faces south.
A KEN house sits to the northeast and faces southwest.
A CHEN house sits to the east and faces west.
A SUN house sits to the southeast and faces northwest.

Consequently, you are likely to be extremely happy if you are a Li and your front door faces north. However, you would also be happy in a house where the front door faced south, west, or northwest as these are all directions that harmonize well with people belonging to the West Four Houses group.

Now that you know your personal trigram, you can find out your positive and negative directions by looking at Figure 10A. There are four positive and four negative directions in every home. In a Tui home, for instance, which faces east and sits to the west, the positive directions are west, southwest, northeast, and northwest. The negative directions are east, north, southeast, and south.

Positive Directions

It is a good idea to face one of your four favorable directions when doing anything important, such as negotiating a deal or signing papers.

Fortunately, there is an easy way of determining your fortunate locations. If your trigram belongs to the East Four Houses group all four of the east directions are good for you (south, north, east, and southeast). If your trigram belongs to the West Four Houses all four of the west directions are likely to be good for you (northwest, southwest, northeast, and west).

Ideally, your front door should face one of your positive directions, as should your bedroom door and the door to the oven.

House	Chien	K'un	Ken	Tui	Li	K'an	Chen	Sun
Sitting towards	NW	SW	NE	W	S	N	E	SE
Positive Directions								
1. Prime	NW	SW	NE	W	S	N	E	SE
2. Health	NE	W	NW	SW	SE	E	N	S
3. Longevity	SW	NW	W	NE	N	S	SE	E
4. Prosperity	W	NE	SW	NW	E	SE	S	N
Negative Directions								
5. Death	S	N	SE	E	NW	SW	W	NE
6. Disaster	SE	E	S	N	NE	W	SW	NW
7. Six Shar	N	S	E	SE	SW	NW	NE	W
8. Five Ghosts	E	SE	N	S	W	NE	NW	SW

Figure 10A: Positive and Negative Directions

Prime

The prime location is a good one, and is always the direction that the house sits toward. It is commonly known as *Fu Wei* (which means "good life"). It is related to happiness and contentment. This part of the house is well suited for bedrooms. However, it is believed that if your bedroom is situated here you will have more male descendants than female ones. People in management positions can benefit by having their desks face their Prime direction.

Health

The health location is commonly known as *Tien Yi* (which means "celestial doctor"). This area generates vitality and good health. It is an excellent location for the master bedroom. It is also a good position for the dining room as the Health location also encourages good friends into our lives. It is believed to be extremely beneficial to have the oven door facing this direction. If you are experiencing ill health, it is a good idea to orient your bed towards the Health direction.

Longevity

The longevity location is commonly known as *Nien Yi* (which means "a long life with many descendants"). This area creates peace, harmony, and good health. It is related particularly to close family relationships. It is a good place for the bedrooms of elderly people, and is also a good position for the dining room or family room. This location should be stimulated whenever there are problems between family members.

Prosperity

This is the most auspicious location in the home. It is commonly called *Sheng Chi* (which means "generating good ch'i"). It represents forward progress, enthusiasm, energy, and financial success. This is a good location for the front door, the kitchen door, the study, and any location where the household accounts are attended to. Financial prospects improve when this location is stimulated. In fact, it is believed that if this part of the house is looked after, the occupants will ultimately achieve great wealth.

The prosperity direction is your most important direction. Your success is assured if you can manage to orient the most important things of your life in this direction, while at the same time avoiding shars. You can do this by having your bed point in this direction, by having your front door opening onto it, and by traveling to work in this direction.

Negative Directions

All of the negative directions are good places for the toilet as the negative ch'i can be "flushed" away.

Death

The Death location is the worst location in your home, and is the worst possible position for your front door. It is believed that your family will suffer ill health and loss of money and reputation if the front door faces this direction. This location is known as *Chueh Ming,* which means "total catastrophe."

Disaster

The Disaster location is related to disputes, anger, aggression, and legal problems. It is commonly known as *Ho Hai,* which means "accidents and danger." It is a good location for a pantry, storeroom, or toilet. If your bed points in this direction, you are likely to suffer a series of small mishaps.

Six Shar

The Six Shar location is related to procrastination, scandal, legal problems, and loss. It is commonly known as *Lui Shar,* which means "six deaths." This is a good location for the kitchen or toilet.

Five Ghosts

The Five Ghosts location relates to fire, theft, and financial problems. It is also related to squabbles and arguments. It is known as *Wu Kuei,* which means "five ghosts." If your front door faces this direction you are likely to suffer from fire and theft.

Your Front Door

For easy reference, here are the best directions for your front door to face:

If you are a KAN . . .

. . . the south direction means that you will do well financially.

. . . the southeast direction means that you will have many descendants.

If you are a K'UN . . .

. . . the northwest direction makes for a long and happy marriage.

. . . the northeast or west makes for fame, honor and recognition.

If you are a CHEN . . .

. . . the southeast direction means rapid promotion and obedient children.

. . . the south or north directions mean wealth will come with little effort.

If you are a SUN . . .

. . . the east direction means that your children will do well at school.

. . . the south or north means that you will do well financially and your descendants will benefit from your hard work.

If you are a CHIEN . . .

. . . the southwest means that you will do well financially.

. . . the northeast or west means that the fortune you make will last for several generations.

If you are a TUI . . .

. . . the northeast means your fortunes will steadily improve.

. . . the northwest and southwest means that you will benefit financially, and make the wealth increase.

If you are a KEN . . .

. . . the west direction makes for a happy home life and many descendants.

. . . the northwest and southwest directions means that your life will be rich in every way.

If you are a L1 . . .

. . . the north direction means that you will do well financially.

. . . the east and southeast directions mean that your children will do well academically.

Using your fortunate directions can help your life in many ways. If you use them at the right times, your progress through life will be smoother, happier, and a great deal easier than it would otherwise be.

11

Putting It All Together

We hold these truths to be self-evident, that all men are created equal, that they are endowed by their Creator with certain unalienable rights, that among these are life, liberty, and the pursuit of happiness.

—The American Declaration of Independence

People ask me to feng shui their homes for many reasons. Usually, it is because they are aware that something is not quite right, but they are not sure what it is. Frequently, people want a feng shui evaluation to improve their financial position, or to attract—or improve—a relationship. Very seldom do people request a feng shui evaluation solely to increase their happiness. However, everybody finds that their lives become richer, happier, and more harmonious after they have made the necessary changes.

I can recall only two instances where people wanted an evaluation to increase their happiness.

The first of these was a middle-aged composer named Stefan who lived with a partner almost twenty-five years younger than him. Monica was an enormous inspiration to him and his output had increased dramatically in the three years they had been together. Their home was pleasant and comfortable and reflected their interests and personalities. They seemed very close and at first glance it looked as if they should have been perfectly happy.

"That's what everyone thinks," Stefan told me, as we sat outside in their beautifully tended garden. "But we're happy only when we're on our own. Every time we go out, people seem to react negatively to us. Maybe it's jealousy, maybe they don't like seeing an older man with a beautiful young woman—we don't know."

During the conversation I learned that Stefan had suffered a great deal of professional jealousy directed at him during his career. He wrote commercial music and had done well financially. His music colleagues considered that he had "sold out" and that what he wrote was not "real" music. This was hurtful to Stefan, but he was used to it.

Monica, a strikingly attractive twenty-five-year-old, is a dress designer. She had won her first award while still in college and had received a great deal of publicity ever since that time. Her business was also doing well, and she was experiencing the same problems that Stefan had.

It did not surprise me that these two talented people had found each other, as they both knew exactly what the other was going through.

"As soon as we started going out together, everything changed," Stefan said. "People thought it was just a sexual thing, and that it would be over in a couple of months. The fact that we've stayed together, and are closer now than ever before, drives people mad. Why can't they leave us alone?"

"They don't like the fact that we're happy," Monica said. "Whenever we go out, we're aware of people talking about us behind our backs. Some even deliberately make comments knowing that we'll hear them."

"Consequently, we've almost become hermits," Stefan said. "We're only truly happy when we're here at home alone."

Their home was a beautiful, ground-level apartment looking out over a harbor. A fountain outside the main entrance of the complex provided abundant ch'i. Entry to the apartment was either through the main lobby area, or by following a path that meandered across a lawn and led directly to a porch outside their living room.

The apartment contained three bedrooms. They shared the master bedroom, and used the other bedrooms to conduct their businesses in. It was a good-sized apartment, but the living room was full of clutter created by the growth of their operations.

"We both tend to use the living room as a work room," Stefan told me. "I can play things to Monica while she is designing, and it seems to help us." He looked around the room. "It's normally much worse than this. We tidied up before you came."

Stefan and Monica really wanted people to stop talking about them behind their backs. They were certain that they were not being paranoid as some people deliberately made snide remarks in their presence.

"We're both doing well in our fields," Stefan said. "And they're both public, newsworthy occupations. So we have to expect less-successful people to try and knock us down. It happens whenever someone succeeds. Look at Salieri and Mozart. He was jealous of Mozart and tried to pull him down to his level. It's not that kind of thing we're concerned about, but the comments people make about us and our relationship. I know I'm old enough to be Monica's father, but I love her and she loves me. I guess we'll always be the subject of gossip, but this has gone too far."

"If we can reduce the negative comments, would you be happier?" I asked.

"We'd be so happy we wouldn't know what to do!" Monica exclaimed.

I started my assessment by walking through their apartment (see Figure 11A). It was well-lit and received sunlight all day long. While standing at the north-facing front door, I could see through the glass doors at the end of the living room and out to the harbor beyond. This is normally a negative factor, as the beneficial ch'i coming in the front door would immediately disappear out through the back door. However, in this instance, more ch'i was coming in from the large sliding-glass doors than from the front door. A large chandelier in the middle of the living room attracted ch'i from both entrances and reflected it around the apartment. This acted as a remedy, although in this particular situation, none was required.

The living room was rectangular, with an open-plan kitchen to the right. Fortunately, the kitchen area was not visible from the front door. Stefan and Monica had four

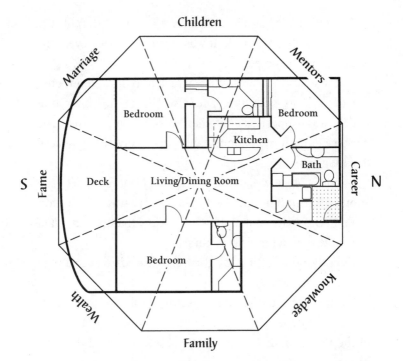

**Figure 11A: Floorplan of
Stefan and Monica's apartment**

stools around a curving eating area, but there was no dining room table.

"We eat out most of the time," Stefan explained. "We do
virtually no entertaining at home."

"That's because the living room's usually in too much of a
muddle," Monica put in.

Stefan put his arm around her. "That's true, but it's more
because we're both busy. We don't have time to cook."

A comfortable leather lounge suite occupied the third of the room nearest the deck. It was arranged so that everyone who sat in it had a pleasant view of the harbor.

To the left was Stefan's office, which also opened out onto the deck. This bedroom, and also the master bedroom, which was opposite, contained ensuite bathrooms. The master bedroom was comfortable and received sunlight all day long.

Monica's office was to the right of the front door, between another bathroom and the kitchen. This was the darkest room in the apartment and had a window that looked out at the parking area for visitors' cars.

I lightly drew a three-by-three magic square over a plan of their apartment.

"Your office is in the Wealth sector," I told Stefan. "This is excellent, as it is where you do most of your work. A third of the living room is in the Fame sector. It's good that you have your lounge suite here as you can enhance your reputation by entertaining small groups of people in this part of your apartment. You also should display some of your awards and photographs in this area."

Stefan and Monica exchanged glances.

"We don't display anything like that," Monica said. "We thought it might increase people's envy."

I shook my head. "Not in this part of your home. You don't need to display everything. Maybe you could choose one thing each, something that you are really proud of."

We moved into the master bedroom. "This could not be better sited," I said. "This is the Marriage sector and is perfect for close relationships. The room is well-lit and looks bright and cheerful. The only negative factor is the ensuite, which sends negative ch'i into the bedroom."

"What can we do about that?" Monica asked.

"I'd keep the door closed and put a mirror on the outside of the door. Because a large mirror would reflect the bed, which is not good from a feng shui point of view, I'd use a small, round mirror, and have it placed reasonably high on the door—high enough so that you could stand in front of it and brush your hair, for instance."

I led the way back through to Stefan's office.

"Here is the problem area," I said, indicating the ensuite bathroom. "This bathroom is in the Family sector. This relates to friends."

Monica laughed. "Are our friendships all going down the toilet?"

I nodded. "In a sense, yes. This room needs more rectifying than the other ensuite. Ideally, this room should totally disappear. That's not practical, so we can symbolically make it vanish by having a mirror on the outside of the door."

"Just as we'll do in the bedroom?"

"You can have a much larger mirror in here, as there is no bed to worry about. You also should have mirrors on two opposite walls to make the entire room symbolically vanish. Mirrors on all four walls would be even better. Finally, you should use this particular bathroom as little as possible."

Stefan shrugged his shoulders. "No problem. We'll stop using it."

We moved back to the living room and stood in the center of the room.

"This is your Good Luck or Spiritual sector," I told them. "You are both obviously using this area, which is perfect, and the chandelier here sends ch'i everywhere." I indicated the stools by the kitchen. "It's good to enjoy meals here together, too."

I indicated the kitchen. "The kitchen, and the ensuite beyond, are in the Children sector."

"So any children are being flushed away, too?"

"That's right. This is a negative placement if you want children."

They both shook their heads. "I've got a grown up family," Stefan said. "And Monica wants to focus on her career. So we've no plans for children, not at present, anyway."

"Your Knowledge area is in the apartment next door," I told them, indicating the part that was missing from their apartment on the plan. "You are symbolically missing that sector in your home. That means that you should remedy this by activating the Knowledge area of a room inside the apartment. I would be inclined to do that in your office, Stefan. You could have a bookcase just to the left of the door inside your office."

"Your entrance lobby and bathroom are both in the Career sector. This is actually not as bad as it sounds. You cannot see the bathroom from the front door. Anyone coming to the front door will see part of your living room and will then look out at your magnificent view beyond. This symbolizes success and forward progress. The only thing I'd suggest is—"

"Keep the bathroom door shut," Monica interjected.

"Yes, I'd do that. I'd also keep the toilet lid down, as well. What I'd suggest is that you keep this part of the apartment well-lit, as this area gets no direct sunlight."

Finally, we looked at Monica's office. Both her desk and designing easel faced the door. Large modern light fittings ensured that plenty of ch'i would flow into what would otherwise have been a dark and gloomy room.

"This is your Mentors sector," I told them. "With all this light in here, you should have no problems in attracting helpful people to you."

Monica nodded. "We've never had problems in that regard."

I visited them again two weeks later to make sure that the remedies I suggested had been put into place correctly. A beaming Monica opened the door and led me in.

"It's working!" she said. "I can't believe how everything changed virtually overnight."

Stefan came out of his office and joined us. After pouring some drinks, he made a toast to feng shui. "You know," he said, "I was skeptical. Some friends had had their place looked at, and claimed that it changed their lives. So, I thought, it couldn't hurt. But I never expected the changes to be so quick, or dramatic. We couldn't be happier now."

Stefan and Monica were rich, successful and famous, and living in a beautiful apartment in the best part of town. They had everything money could buy, but were not truly happy until they had made a few simple adjustments using feng shui.

The other instance where someone wanted to become happier could not have been more different.

Sylvia lived on her own in a bungalow that she had inherited from her parents. She was in her late thirties and had lived in the same house for all of her life.

"My father died when I was ten," she told me. "I can't remember too much about him, although he was a kind, loving father. When he died, Mum became depressed and, in some ways, I don't think she ever came out of it. She was an invalid for the last seven years of her life, and I nursed her here at home. She died almost two years ago."

Sylvia's job involved arranging the Customs' clearances for an importing company. She had worked for them ever since leaving high school.

"I didn't go to college," she explained. "Mum wasn't in good health, and I thought it was better to stay home and look after her. I work just ten minutes from home, and I was able to pop home at lunchtime to see if Mum was all right."

Sylvia had considered herself happy as long as her mother was alive. However, she now found herself alone, and virtually friendless. She had had a few boyfriends in her teenage years, but had rebuffed all advances since then.

"I really want a relationship," she told me. "It would have to be the right man, of course. He'd have to be understanding and gentle, as I am totally inexperienced in that area. I'd also like a few friends. I know lots of people through work, but none of them are really friends."

"Would you be happy if you found the right relationship and made some friends?"

Sylvia nodded. "I think so. There's nothing else I need. I hate living with the feeling that something is missing."

Sylvia's home was modest but looked attractive from the outside. The grounds were well-tended, and flower beds adorned either side of the curving path that led to the front door. It was a wooden house that had recently been painted.

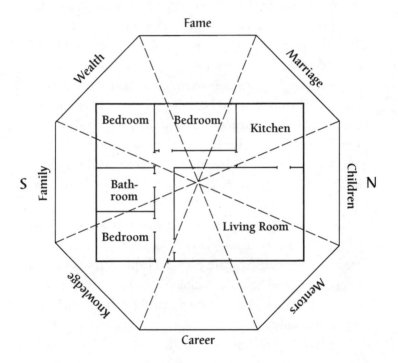

**Figure 11B: Floorplan of
Sylvia's apartment**

From the front door I could see a hallway and the entrance to the living room. Sylvia nervously ushered me in and asked me to have a seat. The walls of the living room were panelled, making the room appear dark and gloomy.

She insisted on making me a pot of tea and as we sipped tea together she told me about her life and how things had changed since the death of her mother.

I explained something about feng shui and then asked her to show me the house. The house had three bedrooms, but one was being used as a dining room (Figure 11B, page 119). This room was at the end of a shar created by a hallway leading from the front door.

Two major problems were immediately apparent. Sylvia's kitchen was in the Marriage sector, and her Family sector was in the bathroom. No wonder she was having problems in making friends and finding a partner.

Sylvia slept in a bedroom that was in the Wealth sector, and the other bedroom, in the Knowledge sector, had been her mother's room.

After this inspection, we sat down again in the living room and I drew a floor plan of her home and placed a three-by-three magic square over it. I explained what each sector meant, and how she could activate any of them if she wished. Nor surprisingly, the two that she chose were Marriage and Family.

"We have a problem with both of these," I told her. "Fortunately, in feng shui, there is a remedy for pretty well everything, and we will need to do something to activate these areas. Your Marriage area is in the kitchen. This is not a good placement as it means that some of your good fortune goes down the drain. However, it is a room where you spend a great deal of time, and we can put something romantic in here to help activate a relationship. It needs to be something that makes you think of love and romance whenever you see it. For instance, I have a friend who used two white candles to symbolize two people. Other people I know have hung up romantic posters."

Sylvia nodded. "I have something that should work."

"Good. Now we also need to make a few changes in your bedroom. I notice that you have a single bed."

"It's what I've always had."

"That's fine, but it also symbolically says that you'd rather sleep on your own. You should replace it with a double bed, and make sure that it can be accessed from both sides. Doing that will help you attract a partner. You also need to activate the Marriage sector of your bedroom, which is the area diagonally to the right from your door. Again, you need something that you feel is romantic. It can be something small—there's no need for anything large or ornate.

"Now, let's move on to your Family sector. As it is in the bathroom, it conflicts with your desire to attract friends. Fortunately, there is a simple remedy. You can symbolically make that room disappear by using mirrors on opposite walls inside the room, and by having a mirror on the outside of the door. You should also keep the door of this room closed.

"However, having done that, you will also need to activate the Family sector in one of the other rooms. I think your living room would be the best place for this. This is also the perfect place to display photographs of relatives or friends.

"It would also be a good idea to have something metal-lic in this area." (This is because Sylvia was born in 1962 and belongs to the Water element. Metal, of course, helps create Water.)

Sylvia is a K'un and lives in a Tui house. This is good because these trigrams both belong to the East Four Houses.

However, there are a number of problems with her home. Her front door, for instance, is in the Six Shar sector, indicating the potential for legal problems, or even a scandal. Her mother's bedroom is also in this sector, and it is fortunate that Sylvia decided not to move into this room.

Her Prosperity sector is in the kitchen. This is not necessarily bad, as Sylvia spends a great deal of time in the kitchen and the room is well lit. The dining room (formerly a bedroom) is in the Prime sector. As Sylvia belongs to the Water element, this would be the perfect place in the house for an aquarium. The Longevity sector takes up part of the living room. It would be better if it was in the dining room, but as the living room is usually a place where all the occupants spend time, this is a good placement.

Sylvia's bedroom could not be better sited. The Health area is the best placement for the master bedroom. Of course, the bedroom that her mother used was generally considered the master bedroom, but as Sylvia now lives in the house on her own, the room she sleeps in is considered to be the master bedroom.

The toilet is perfectly sited in the Five Ghosts sector.

The Disaster sector takes up part of the living room. Sylvia would be advised to move her lounge suite out of this part of the room, as any guests would be likely to argue.

Sylvia wrote down virtually everything I told her and said that she would start making changes right away. I told her to make any changes slowly. By doing this, she would be able to gauge the effect each change had on her situation.

She called me a month later to tell me that during the previous week two men had asked her out. As no one had asked her out for several years, she was bewildered and concerned that she may have made too many changes, too quickly. I assured her that this was not the case, but accepted her invitation to come and see what she had done.

She had replaced her single bed with a double one, and in the Marriage sector of her bedroom had an ornament made out of magnetic metal hearts. As they stuck to each other, she was able to change their positions and create as many different designs as she wished.

In the kitchen was a large poster showing a large, red heart. Inside it, in large letters, was the message: "I love you!" In the Marriage sector of her living room she had a heart-shaped picture frame, containing a cartoon drawing of a young married couple. It was easy to tell that hearts represented love and romance for Sylvia.

She had also installed four large mirrors inside the bathroom, and a heart-shaped mirror hung on the outside of the door.

"Do you think I've overdone the love part?" she asked.

"Not at all," I assured her. "I'm certain that from now on, you'll be an extremely popular lady!"

In fact, it took Sylvia less than a year to find the right partner. He seems perfect for her. He is in his early forties and is an accountant for a bank. He has been on his own for ten years. His wife died tragically in a car accident. I am extremely happy that Sylvia was able to bring so much happiness into her life simply by changing the energies of her home.

Although these are the only evaluations I have done where the sole aim was greater happiness, in effect, the purpose of every evaluation is to enable the client to enjoy more happiness, contentment, and abundance in every part of his or her life.

12

Conclusion

Who fails to enjoy his happy moments cannot be called lucky; but the man who feels happy even while undergoing difficulties is the real cultivated man.

—Chinese proverb

I hope that this book will encourage you to use the principles of feng shui to achieve greater happiness and contentment in every part of your life. For thousands of years feng shui has helped people achieve their goals, whatever they may be.

Happiness is an essential part of life. Many years ago I knew a man who suffered from depression. Everything would go well in his life for a long time and then, usually quite suddenly, he would fall into a major depression. He and his family would suffer enormously until, just as mysteriously, he would climb out of his depression again and be able to carry on with his life. This illness totally ruined his life, and that of the people he loved. It made me realize that happiness is a precious gift, and that anything that can increase our happiness is extremely worthwhile.

The Chinese have three house gods, known as the Star Gods. These are Fu'k, Lu'k, and Sau, the gods of happiness, affluence, and longevity. You have probably seen porcelain statues in Chinese restaurants of these venerable old gentlemen standing together, bestowing blessings on the owner, staff, and customers.

Fu'k is a tall, distinguished looking man wearing court clothes and carrying a scepter. Lu'k wears similar clothes and carries a small boy. (The small boy symbolizes the importance the ancient Chinese had for sons and grandsons to carry on the family line.) Sau is the easiest to recognize, as he has a bald head and a long white beard. He carries a long staff and a peach.

These statues symbolize the desires of the Chinese. Fu'k represents happiness and good fortune. Lu'k represents prosperity, a happy family life, and a successful career. Sau symbolizes a long life.

These figures represent a silent affirmation, depicting all the requirements of a happy and successful life. By using feng shui, we can activate all of these blessings. In this book, we have focused on happiness. However, I hope that reading this may stimulate you to study more books on the subject. I have listed a number of good books on feng shui in the Suggested Reading section (see page 143).

Some people go overboard and make dozens of changes at once. It is natural to want to do everything immediately, but it is better to activate one area at a time. By doing this, you will be able to evaluate the results that each change brings. You will find that some changes bring dramatic results, while others are more subtle. Take your time, decide which areas you wish to activate first, make one or two changes, and then pause for a few weeks. Be alert for any changes that occur, and then make one or two more. It might take a few months to change everything you wish, but by doing it this way you will have a clear idea of exactly what things created certain results.

I hope you have enjoyed this book, and hope it will encourage you to continue with your studies in this fascinating subject. I wish you great happiness.

Appendix

Elements and Signs for the Years 1900 to 2000

Element	Sign	Year
Metal	Rat	Jan. 31, 1900 to Feb. 18, 1901
Metal	Ox	Feb. 19, 1901 to Feb. 7, 1902
Water	Tiger	Feb. 8, 1902 to Jan. 28, 1903
Water	Rabbit	Jan. 29, 1903 to Feb. 15, 1904
Wood	Dragon	Feb. 16, 1904 to Feb. 3, 1905
Wood	Snake	Feb. 4, 1905 to Jan. 24, 1906
Fire	Horse	Jan. 25, 1906 to Feb. 12, 1907
Fire	Sheep	Feb. 13, 1907 to Feb. 1, 1908
Earth	Monkey	Feb. 2, 1908 to Jan. 21, 1909
Earth	Rooster	Jan. 22, 1909 to Feb. 9, 1910
Metal	Dog	Feb. 10, 1910 to Jan. 29, 1911
Metal	Boar	Jan. 30, 1911 to Feb. 17, 1912
Water	Rat	Feb. 18, 1912 to Feb. 5, 1913
Water	Ox	Feb. 6, 1913 to Jan. 25, 1914
Wood	Tiger	Jan. 26, 1914 to Feb. 13, 1915

Wood	Rabbit	Feb. 14, 1915 to Feb. 2, 1916
Fire	Dragon	Feb. 3, 1916 to Jan. 22, 1917
Fire	Snake	Jan. 23, 1917 to Feb. 10, 1918
Earth	Horse	Feb. 11, 1918 to Jan. 31, 1919
Earth	Sheep	Feb. 1, 1919 to Feb. 19, 1920
Metal	Monkey	Feb. 20, 1920 to Feb. 7, 1921
Metal	Rooster	Feb. 8, 1921 to Jan. 27, 1922
Water	Dog	Jan. 28, 1922 to Feb. 15, 1923
Water	Boar	Feb. 16, 1923 to Feb. 4, 1924
Wood	Rat	Feb. 5, 1924 to Jan. 24, 1925
Wood	Ox	Jan. 25, 1925 to Feb. 12, 1926
Fire	Tiger	Feb. 13, 1926 to Feb. 1, 1927
Fire	Rabbit	Feb. 2, 1927 to Jan. 22, 1928
Earth	Dragon	Jan. 23, 1928 to Feb. 9, 1929
Earth	Snake	Feb. 10, 1929 to Jan. 29, 1930
Metal	Horse	Jan. 30, 1930 to Feb. 16, 1931
Metal	Sheep	Feb. 17, 1931 to Feb. 5, 1932
Water	Monkey	Feb. 6, 1932 to Jan. 25, 1933
Water	Rooster	Jan. 26, 1933 to Feb. 13, 1934
Wood	Dog	Feb. 14, 1934 to Feb. 3, 1935
Wood	Boar	Feb. 4, 1935 to Jan. 23, 1936
Fire	Rat	Jan. 24, 1936 to Feb. 10, 1937
Fire	Ox	Feb. 11, 1937 to Jan. 30, 1938
Earth	Tiger	Jan. 31, 1938 to Feb. 18, 1939
Earth	Rabbit	Feb. 19, 1939 to Feb. 7, 1940
Metal	Dragon	Feb. 8, 1940 to Jan. 26, 1941
Metal	Snake	Jan. 27, 1941 to Feb. 14, 1942
Water	Horse	Feb. 15, 1942 to Feb. 4, 1943
Water	Sheep	Feb. 5, 1943 to Jan. 24, 1944
Wood	Monkey	Jan. 25, 1944 to Feb. 12, 1945

Wood	Rooster	Feb. 13, 1945 to Feb. 1, 1946
Fire	Dog	Feb. 2, 1946 to Jan. 21, 1947
Fire	Boar	Jan. 22, 1947 to Feb. 9, 1948
Earth	Rat	Feb. 10, 1948 to Jan. 28, 1949
Earth	Ox	Jan. 29, 1949 to Feb. 16, 1950
Metal	Tiger	Feb. 17, 1950 to Feb. 5, 1951
Metal	Rabbit	Feb. 6, 1951 to Jan. 26, 1952
Water	Dragon	Jan. 27, 1952 to Feb. 13, 1953
Water	Snake	Feb. 14, 1953 to Feb. 2, 1954
Wood	Horse	Feb. 3, 1954 to Jan. 23, 1955
Wood	Sheep	Jan. 24, 1955 to Feb. 11, 1956
Fire	Monkey	Feb. 12, 1956 to Jan. 30, 1957
Fire	Rooster	Jan. 31, 1957 to Feb. 17, 1958
Earth	Dog	Feb. 18, 1958 to Feb. 7, 1959
Earth	Boar	Feb. 8, 1959 to Jan. 27, 1960
Metal	Rat	Jan. 28, 1960 to Feb. 14, 1961
Metal	Ox	Feb. 15, 1961 to Feb. 4, 1962
Water	Tiger	Feb. 5, 1962 to Jan. 24, 1963
Water	Rabbit	Jan. 25, 1963 to Feb. 12, 1964
Wood	Dragon	Feb. 13, 1964 to Feb. 1, 1965
Wood	Snake	Feb. 2, 1965 to Jan. 20, 1966
Fire	Horse	Jan. 21, 1966 to Feb. 8, 1967
Fire	Sheep	Feb. 9, 1967 to Jan. 29, 1968
Earth	Monkey	Jan. 30, 1968 to Feb. 16, 1969
Earth	Rooster	Feb. 17, 1969 to Feb. 5, 1970
Metal	Dog	Feb. 6, 1970 to Jan. 26, 1971
Metal	Boar	Jan. 27, 1971 to Jan. 15, 1972
Water	Rat	Jan. 16, 1972 to Feb. 2, 1973
Water	Ox	Feb. 3, 1973 to Jan. 22, 1974
Wood	Tiger	Jan. 23, 1974 to Feb. 10, 1975

Wood	Rabbit	Feb. 11, 1975 to Jan. 30, 1976
Fire	Dragon	Jan. 31, 1976 to Feb. 17, 1977
Fire	Snake	Feb. 18, 1977 to Feb. 6, 1978
Earth	Horse	Feb. 7, 1978 to Jan. 27, 1979
Earth	Sheep	Jan. 28, 1979 to Feb. 15, 1980
Metal	Monkey	Feb. 16, 1980 to Feb. 4, 1981
Metal	Rooster	Feb. 5, 1981 to Jan. 24, 1982
Water	Dog	Jan. 25, 1982 to Feb. 12, 1983
Water	Boar	Feb. 13, 1983 to Feb. 1, 1984
Wood	Rat	Feb. 2, 1984 to Feb. 19, 1985
Wood	Ox	Feb. 20, 1985 to Feb. 8, 1986
Fire	Tiger	Feb. 9, 1986 to Jan. 28, 1987
Fire	Rabbit	Jan. 29, 1987 to Feb. 16, 1988
Earth	Dragon	Feb. 17, 1988 to Feb. 5, 1989
Earth	Snake	Feb. 6, 1989 to Jan. 26, 1990
Metal	Horse	Jan. 27, 1990 to Feb. 14, 1991
Metal	Sheep	Feb. 15, 1991 to Feb. 3, 1992
Water	Monkey	Feb. 4, 1992 to Jan. 22, 1993
Water	Rooster	Jan. 23, 1993 to Feb. 9, 1994
Wood	Dog	Feb. 10, 1994 to Jan. 30, 1995
Wood	Boar	Jan. 31, 1995 to Feb. 18, 1996
Fire	Rat	Feb. 19, 1996 to Feb. 6, 1997
Fire	Ox	Feb. 7, 1997 to Jan. 27, 1998
Earth	Tiger	Jan. 28, 1998 to Feb. 15, 1999
Earth	Rabbit	Feb. 16, 1999 to Feb. 4, 2000
Metal	Dragon	Feb. 5, 2000

Notes

Introduction

1. Joseph Spence, *Anecdotes* (London, 1756).
2. Lin Yutang, *The Importance of Living* (London: William Heinemann Limited, 1937), 133.
3. Lin Yutang, *The Importance of Living,* 140 – 141.

Chapter One

1. Benjamin Disraeli, *Contarini Fleming* (London, 1832)
2. Confucius, quoted in *The Spirit of the Chinese Character* by Barbara Aria with Russell Eng Gon (San Francisco: Chronicle Books, 1992). 72.
3. Further information on the history and development of the three-by-three magic square can be found in *Numerology Magic* by Richard Webster (St. Paul: Llewellyn Publications, 1995).

Chapter Four

1. Lillian Too, *Feng Shui* (Malaysia: Konsep Lagenda Sdn Bhd., 1993), 33.
2. Frena Bloomfield, *The Book of Chinese Beliefs* (London: Arrow Books Limited, 1983), 23.
3. Richard Webster, *Feng Shui for Beginners* (St. Paul: Llewellyn Publications, 1997), 8.
4. Ong Hean-Tatt, *Secrets of Ancient Chinese Art of Motivation* (Malaysia: Pelanduk Publications (M) Sdn Bhd, 1994), 51.

Chapter Seven

1. Joseph Campbell quoted in *Altars Made Easy* by Peg Streep (New York: HarperSanFrancisco, 1997), 1.
2. Richard Webster, *Omens, Oghams and Oracles* (St. Paul: Llewellyn Publications, 1995), 39 – 41.
3. Richard Webster, *Spirit Guides and Angel Guardians* (St. Paul: Llewellyn Publications, 1998), 123 – 129.

Chapter Eight

1. Richard Webster, *Feng Shui for Beginners,* xxiv.
2. J. Dyer Ball, *Things Chinese* (Singapore: Graham Brasch (Pte) Limited, 1989. Originally published in 1903.), 245.
3. Richard Webster, *Feng Shui in the Garden* (St. Paul, MN: Llewellyn Publications, 1999).

4. Ong Hean-Tatt, *Chinese Animal Symbolisms* (Malaysia: Pelanduk Publications (M) Sdn. Bhd., 1993), 246.

5. Karen Kingston, *Creating Sacred Space with Feng Shui* (New York, NY: Broadway Books, 1997), 125.

Chapter Nine

1. Not everyone believes that Lao-tzu actually existed. The name Lao-tzu means "venerable philosopher," and the *Tao Te Ching* may well have been a compilation of writings by different people. In his book, *Religions of China* (San Francisco: Harper and Row, 1986) Daniel L. Overmyer says that the author of the *Tao Te Ching* is unknown (page 121).

2. Walter T. Stace, *The Teachings of the Mystics* (New York, NY: New American Library, 1960), 102.

3. Chinghua Tang, *A Treasury of China's Wisdom* (Beijing: Foreign Languages Press, 1996), 387.

4. Encyclopaedia Britannica (Chicago, IL: Encyclopaedia Britannica, Inc., 15th edition, 1983) Volume 10, 680.

5. Barbara Aria with Russell Eng Gon, *The Spirit of the Chinese Character,* 19.

6. Encyclopaedia Britannica, Volume 10, 681.

7. Lin Yutang, *The Wisdom of China* (London: Michael Joseph Limited, 1944), 242.

8. J. Dyer Ball, *Things Chinese* (Singapore: Graham Brasch (Pte) Limited, 1989. Originally published in 1903), 157.

Glossary

Ch'i—the universal life force that is found in all things. It is continually being created and dissipated. Anything beautiful in nature creates ch'i. Any task performed perfectly also creates ch'i.

Compass School—There are two main schools of feng shui, the Form School and the Compass School The Compass School uses the pa-kua, the eight trigrams, and Chinese astrology to evaluate the feng shui of any location. For the last hundred years, most feng shui practitioners have used a combination of the two schools to make their assessments.

Confucius (551 – 479 B.C.E.) developed a concept of moral and social order that symbolized a perfect world with everything in its correct place. It also symbolizes righteousness, good manners, fairness, and even faith.

Confucianism is a philosophy that includes personal ethics, empathy, and a deep compassion for others. He advocated the Golden Mean, which meant following a middle path, and avoiding extremes, excesses, or overindulgence. Confucius believed that by training people to be honest and compassionate, the world would be a much happier and more harmonious place.

Cycle of Destruction—The five elements of Chinese astrology can be arranged in a number of different ways. In the destructive cycle, each element overpowers and dominates the element that follows it in the cycle. In this cycle Fire melts Metal. Metal destroys Wood. Wood drains from the Earth. Earth can dam and block Water. Water puts out Fire.

Cycle of Production—In the productive cycle, each element helps to create and support the element that follows it. Consequently, Wood burns to create Fire. Fire produces Earth. Earth produces Metal. Metal liquefies, which symbolically creates Water. Water nurtures and creates Wood.

East Four Houses—The East Four Houses of Li, K'an, Chen and Sun are derived from the eight directions indicated by the eight-sided pa-kua. They can be summarized this way:

House	Back Door Faces	Element
Li	South	Fire
K'an	North	Water
Chen	East	Wood
Sun	Southeast	Wood

Feng Shui—means "wind and water." It is the art and practice of living in harmony with the earth. If we live in harmony with the earth, we can enjoy a life full of happiness, contentment, and abundance.

Feng shui has a history that goes back some five thousand years. Until recently, it was practiced only in the East, but in recent times it has spread around the world, and today it is more popular than at any other time in its history.

Five Elements—Feng shui uses the five elements of Chinese astrology. These are Wood, Fire, Earth, Metal and Water. Each element has its own distinct energy and the different combinations of the elements play a significant role in feng shui. The different elements can harmonize (as in the Cycle of Production) or oppose each other (as in the Cycle of Destruction).

Form School—the original version of feng shui that predates the compass. A practitioner of the Form School looks at the contours of the landscape to make his assessments.

Lao-tze lived about 570 B.C.E. and is considered to be the father of Taoism. The main thrust of his philosophy was to let things take their own course because everything would always work out in the end without the need for effort. His ideas were recorded in the *Tao Te Ching*.

Magic Square—a series of numbers arranged inside a grid where all the horizontal, vertical, and diagonal rows add up to the same number. Magic squares have been popular in China for thousands of years. The magic square that was found in the markings of a tortoise shell by Wu of Hsia formed the basis of feng shui, the I Ching, Chinese astrology, and Chinese numerology.

Pa-kua—an eight-sided shape that usually has either a mirror or the yin-yang symbol in the center. The eight trigrams from the I Ching are arranged around the central object.

Pa-kuas are frequently found hanging above the doors of Chinese homes as symbols of protection or as lucky talismans. They are also used to send back shars that affect the front door of the home.

Remedies—sometimes known as "cures," they are anything that eliminates or blocks the effects of a shar. They are also used to remedy any imbalances of the five elements in any given situation. A wall erected to block a shar would be considered a remedy.

Shars—are often known as "poison arrows." They are lines of negative energy that bring the potential for misfortune and bad luck. They are created in two ways. Any straight line heading directly towards you would be considered a shar. A straight road heading towards a house facing a T-junction would be considered a shar. Angles, such as two walls of a house, create arrows that adversely affect anything they are pointing towards.

Silent Affirmations—An affirmation is a short phrase or sentence that is repeated over and over again to instill positive thoughts into the mind. A famous example by Emil Coué is: "Every day, in every way, I am getting better and better." In the East, people use silent affirmations. These are objects that immediately make us think of a positive thought or saying. Gold fish, for example, make Asian people think of upward progress and prosperity. A small metal container holding a few coins sitting in the Wealth sector of a desk would make the occupant think of money every time he or she sees it.

Trigrams—The eight trigrams comprise every possible combination of straight and broken lines that can be made from three lines. The straight lines are known as yang lines and represent male energy. The broken lines are yin and represent female energy. The hexagrams of the I Ching are made up of two trigrams, one on top of the other.

West Four Houses—The West Four Houses of Chien, K'un, Ken, and Tui represent four of the eight directions indicated by the eight-sided pa-kua. They can best be summarized by this chart:

House	Back Door Faces	Element
Chien	Northwest	Metal
K'un	Southwest	Earth
Ken	Northeast	Earth
Tui	West	Metal

Yin and Yang—represent opposites in the Taoist philosophy. It was never defined; rather lists of opposites were created to represent yin and yang. For example: black is yin and yang is white. Night is yin and day is yang. Other examples are: female and male, low and high, front and back, cold and hot. The concept originally came from observation of two sides of a mountain. The shady, northern side was yin, and the sunny, southern slopes were yang. This dualistic view of the world is an important part of the feng shui concept.

Suggested Reading

Heann-Tatt, Ong. *The Chinese Pakua*. Malaysia: Pelandul Publications, 1991.

Kehoe, John. *A Vision of Power and Glory*. Vancouver, BC: Zoetic Inc., 1994.

de Kermadec, Jean-Michel Huon. *The Way to Chinese Astrology: The Four Pillars of Destiny*. Translated by N. Derek Poulsen. London: Unwin Paperbacks, 1983.

Kingston, Karen. *Creating Sacred Space with Feng Shui*. London: Judy Piatkus (Publishers) Limited, 1996.

Linn, Denise. *Sacred Space*. New York, NY: Ballantine Books, 1996.

Marfori, Mark D. *Feng Shui: Discover Money, Health and Love*. Santa Monica, CA: Dragon Publishing, 1993.

Simons, T. Raphael. *Feng Shui Step by Step*. New York, NY: Crown Trade Paperbacks, 1996.

Streep, Peg. *Altars Made Easy.* New York, NY: HarperSan-Francisco, 1997.

Too, Lillian. *Feng Shui.* Malaysia: Konsep Lagenda Sdn Bhd., 1993.

Tsuei, Wei. *Roots of Chinese Culture and Medicine.* Malaysia: Pelanduk Publications, 1992.

Webster, Richard. *Feng Shui for Beginners.* St. Paul, MN: Llewellyn Publications, 1997.

———. *101 Feng Shui Tips for the Home.* St. Paul, MN: Llewellyn Publications, 1998.

———. *Feng Shui for Apartment Living.* St. Paul, MN: Llewellyn Publications, 1998.

———. *Feng Shui for Love & Romance.* St. Paul, MN: Llewellyn Publications, 1998.

———. *Feng Shui for the Workplace.* St. Paul, MN: Llewellyn Publications, 1998.

———. *Feng Shui in the Garden.* St. Paul: Llewellyn Publications, 1998.

Wong, Eva. *Feng Shui: The Ancient Wisdom of Harmonious Living for Modern Times.* Boston: Shambhala Publications, Inc., 1996.

Wydra, Nancilee. *Designing Your Happiness.* Torrance, CA: Heian International Inc., 1995.

Index

☽ LOOK FOR THE CRESCENT MOON

Llewellyn publishes hundreds of books on your favorite subjects! To get these exciting books, including the ones on the following pages, check your local bookstore or order them directly from Llewellyn.

ORDER BY PHONE

- Call toll-free within the U.S. and Canada, 1-800-THE MOON
- In Minnesota, call (651) 291-1970
- We accept VISA, MasterCard, and American Express

ORDER BY MAIL

- Send the full price of your order (MN residents add 7% sales tax) in U.S. funds, plus postage & handling to:

  Llewellyn Worldwide
  P.O. Box 64383, Dept. K815-X
  St. Paul, MN 55164–0383, U.S.A.

POSTAGE & HANDLING

(For the U.S., Canada, and Mexico)

- $4.00 for orders $15.00 and under
- $5.00 for orders over $15.00
- No charge for orders over $100.00

We ship UPS in the continental United States. We ship standard mail to P.O. boxes. Orders shipped to Alaska, Hawaii, The Virgin Islands, and Puerto Rico are sent first-class mail. Orders shipped to Canada and Mexico are sent surface mail.

International orders: Airmail—add freight equal to price of each book to the total price of order, plus $5.00 for each non-book item (audio tapes, etc.).

Surface mail—Add $1.00 per item.

Allow 4–6 weeks for delivery on all orders.
Postage and handling rates subject to change.

DISCOUNTS

We offer a 20% discount to group leaders or agents. You must order a minimum of 5 copies of the same book to get our special quantity price.

FREE CATALOG

Get a free copy of our color catalog, **New Worlds of Mind and Spirit**. Subscribe for just $10.00 in the United States and Canada ($30.00 overseas, airmail). Many bookstores carry **New Worlds**—ask for it!

Visit our web site at www.llewellyn.com for more information.

FENG SHUI
FOR BEGINNERS
Successful Living by Design

Richard Webster

Not advancing fast enough in your career? Maybe your desk is located in a "negative position." Wish you had a more peaceful family life? Hang a mirror in your dining room and watch what happens. Is money flowing out of your life rather than into it? You may want to look to the construction of your staircase!

For thousands of years, the ancient art of feng shui has helped people harness universal forces and lead lives rich in good health, wealth and happiness. The basic techniques in *Feng Shui for Beginners* are very simple, and you can put them into place immediately in your home and work environments. Gain peace of mind, a quiet confidence, and turn adversity to your advantage with feng shui remedies.

1-56718-803-6, 240 pp., 5 ¹/₄ x 8, photos, softcover $12.95

101 FENG SHUI TIPS FOR THE HOME
Richard Webster

For thousand of years, people in the Far East have used feng shui to improve their home and family lives and live in harmony with the earth. Certainly, people who practice feng-shui achieve a deep contentment that is denied most others. They usually do well romantically and financially. Architects around the world are beginning to incorporate the concepts of feng shui into their designs. Even people like Donald Trump freely admit to using feng shui.

Now you can make subtle and inexpensive changes to your home that can literally transform your life. If you're in the market for a house, learn what to look for in room design, single level vs. split level, staircases, front door location and more. If you want to improve upon your existing home, find out how its current design may be creating negative energy, and discover simple ways to remedy the situation without the cost of major renovations or remodeling.

Watch your success and spirits soar when you discover:
- How to evaluate the current feng shui energy in your home
- What to do about negative energy coming from neighbors
- How to use fountains or aquariums to attract money
- The best position for the front door
- How to arrange your living room furniture
- Colors to use and avoid for each member of the family

1-56718-809-5, 192 pp., 5 ¼ x 8, charts   **$9.95**

To order, call 1-800-THE MOON
Prices subject to change without notice